from
first date
to chosen
mate

from first date to chosen mate

BRENTON G. YORGASON

Bookcraft
Salt Lake City, Utah

Library of Congress Catalog Card Number: 77-78410
ISBN 0-88494-319-4

5th Printing, 1979

Lithographed in the United States of America
PUBLISHERS PRESS
Salt Lake City, Utah

Contents

Foreword

After reading the manuscript for *From First Date to Chosen Mate,* I am convinced that within these chapters the author has succeeded in communicating both the significance and the substance of relationships in the realms of dating and courtship. This is a book of exceptional practical value, since each chapter is complete within itself yet is but one facet of a multi-sided prism comprising the total dating experience.

In today's society no other single problem crops up with more intensity and frequency than relationships between young men and women. More young people have been "grounded," more hearts have been broken, more parents have nursed ulcers over this one subject than over any other subject in the modern world.

The book is fashioned from the observation and experiences of one man dedicated to teaching youth proper relationships in a complex world. The author brings to this work several years of study, experience, and counseling. His ability to relate to young people today is indeed a rare quality. The advice he gives is sound, strong, and timely. He draws from real people, young and old, and, rather than offering a list of restrictions, gives concrete ways to improve self. The young person, whether dating or not yet dating, the frustrated parent, and those preparing for marriage, will all benefit from the insights contained within these pages.

In this book the imperative message comes through that, in order to find true joy, young people must find those principles upon which the progress of the eternal soul is based, stay strong in those concepts and practices, and endure to the end.

DAN L. BELL

Acknowledgments

I express appreciation to the many who have given of their time and talents in making this book publishable. Special young friends who have assisted in this include Margaret Benson, Cheri Nash, Amy Kipp, Sandy Griffiths, Karen Lloyd, David "Pearl" Paul, Dave Olsen, Peggy Kofford, Jennifer Wilcox, Diana Jensen, Karen Ensign, Cindy Carlson, and Laurel, Sharyn, and Diana Ball. Kathy Ludlow labored long and arduously in typing and editing.

I would like to thank also Elder and Sister Paul H. Dunn for their timely critique and encouragement.

I feel a special sense of appreciation to my dear wife, Margaret, for her constant love and encouragement, and especially for her staying power during the long hours of research and writing.

Finally, I thank all of my special young friends, whose love and lives have inspired this writing.

Chapter 1

The Right One

Jennifer sat painfully in her English class. The Monday before the last big dance of her high school career, and no one had invited her to go. She glanced over at Greg. If only *he* would ask her! If only he would just *notice* her! But he didn't even know she existed as he just sat there, flipping his pencil and gazing wistfully at the newly formed leaves on the trees outside.

The room dissolved into a haze as the well-worn pattern of thought returned. "Greg Wagstaff: senior, seminary president, basketball star, tall, blonde, and with a smile that melts the hearts of all of the senior girls (in fact, of almost every girl in the whole studentbody)." A sigh escaped from Jennifer. "If only I were better-looking and dared to actually *talk* to him. Oh, well, what's the use? He would only shrug me off and think I was weird or something."

Equally oblivious to the charms of English composition, Nate Anderson sat in the back of the room. "Good ol' Nate," he was saying to himself. "Yes, that's all I am, just 'Good ol' Nate,' a guy to haul everyone else around in my V-Dub. Yet no one could care less about me. The girls don't even know I'm alive. Why do guys like Greg get all the breaks? Ah, well, I don't even care anymore! As far as I'm concerned, life's one big drag anyway."

As the week progressed, Jennifer spent much of it in tears. There was no last-minute phone call, and the dance came and went. Her high school career had ended, and during that whole time she had gone on only two dates (other than girls' choice), and those were with two guys who were "nobodies" at school.

Nate left school as disheartened as Jennifer, but for different reasons. He knew he didn't have what it took, so he didn't even consider college or a mission. Instead he got a job driving a truck for an electrical supply company. Incidentally, he never married.

In the responses of Jennifer and Nate we see enacted the two most common tragedies that occur in the lives of young people: Jennifer is a girl who has spent her high school years looking for that dream lover, that "right one" who will come along and take her in his arms and marry her, and with whom she will then live forever in joy and bliss. Nate is a priest in the Aaronic Priesthood who considers himself a dismal failure.

The sad fact is that in our culture there are many Jennifers and Nates who pass through those formative and formidable teenage years without personally recognizing the key to happiness and success in marriage and in life. What is at fault is their "right one" concept. When a person thinks that happiness in life comes only through *finding* the right one, he never fully understands that the real key is in *becoming* the right one.

Now, just exactly what do I mean by that? Well, for one thing I mean that romantic notions are fine in their place, as part of the superstructure, but that the Jennifers who "get their man" *always* find these notions to be a sandy foundation for marriage. And I mean that the Nates wrongly place on others the blame for lack of personal success and happiness. Without realizing it, both types want the fruit without tending the tree. Both want to lean on others in seeking to attain life's greatest offering — happiness. And the

2

plain fact is that this is impossible because it is contrary to the laws of life.

So what should Jennifer and Nate have done? Each should have focused on improving self, on crystallizing ideals, on elevating attitude, on establishing goals — and on tying this package together with a solid, day-by-day effort which will bring these unifying concepts to splendid reality.

Try it! It works in every area of life, including preparation for marriage. As you apply your new approach and effort you will sense that you are accomplishing, achieving, moving upward. You are *becoming*. One of the things you are becoming is the *right one*. And the right one attracts the right one.

It's not too long since I was in high school, so I could quote here from my own experiences. But I'm going to do better than that. I want you to hear from your own generation, from two people who are trying to become the "right one." They share with you some of their feelings and goals and ideals. In the time-honored way, let's hear first from the lady.

"As I sit here and think of how I can express my thoughts to you, I would first like to introduce myself. My name is Karen Lloyd. I am seventeen. I enjoy friends, good times, family, and being involved in everything I can. I'm the kind of person who can really get excited about a big date! I love watching and participating in sports and music.

"This year I have been involved as a member of the Skyline Seminary Council. Because of this, I have looked especially hard at the kind of example I am setting. In evaluating my life to determine whether I was living up to my standards, I began to realize how much impact my standards and beliefs have had on my life. They have truly become the foundation for my whole value system and for what is now important to me. I am grateful that these standards have become one of the strongest forces in my life. High standards

3

have given me a feeling of self-respect. And I have found that when I like and accept myself, it is easier for others to like and accept me.

"Naturally I expect to get married in a few years' time. I have therefore asked myself some questions — questions you might like to ask yourself: What do I want the person I marry to be like? (Describe to yourself as many qualities as you can.) Am I that kind of person? If the answer is no, what changes have to be made? I have done my best to evaluate myself on this basis and make the necessary changes to my standards and to myself.

"I have come to appreciate more than ever before that the future is bought with the present. I know now that we must decide who we want to be today so that we will be the person we want to be tomorrow — the right one!"

Now for the young man.

4

"Hello! I'm David William 'Pearl' Paul. (The 'Pearl' is a name the guys on the basketball team gave me.) I'm eighteen years old, six foot four inches tall, and I weigh in at 165 pounds. Some say I'm a little on the skinny side. I have brown hair, brown eyes, and a brown mustache which no one except me knows is there!

"At school I sing in the concert choir, play as a guard on the Skyline basketball team, and serve on the seminary council. I've already worn braces and gone on my first date. (Thank heavens they're both in the past!)

"These are a few facts about myself that could have been mentioned by anyone who has known me at all. Closer friends or family members most likely would add that I'm very self-confident, or at least I appear to be; and that I have a pretty good sense of humor and at times really enjoy just goofing off. These statements about me are all true, but they give only a superficial picture. I would like now to share the part of me that is seldom seen or heard from — my ideals.

"If you're at all like me, life gets moving so fast at times

that you wonder if it will ever slow down. Between basketball, seminary, school, the Church, family, and friends, it's hard to find time just for myself. On those rare occasions when I do, I like to consider two questions: (1) What is important to me? and (2) What do I want to be like?

"Thinking back to when I was in the eighth grade, I now realize how sheltered I was. I don't know if it was the same for you, but then I was content with just knowing I had good friends and a loving family. I had no great responsibilities, and everything always seemed to fall into place for me.

"Now I am eighteen years old, I can't believe it! That's two years past a driver's license, exactly at voting age, only one year from a mission, and only about four to six years from marriage, leaving home for good, and starting my own family. Suddenly things don't work out as easily as they did when I was younger. There is one thing, though, that has helped me in the past four years, something that has made a great many problems easier and eliminated a considerable number of others. It has to do with the ideals I established for myself when I considered the questions mentioned above.

"Because I had already made some decisions beforehand, the going was really not too difficult. First I made the basic decision that I would not under any circumstances swear, drink, smoke, lie, cheat, or do anything else to destroy my body, mind, or spirit. This decision has made a lot of situations pass by without any problem or hesitation on my part.

"I decided too that I wanted to accomplish certain things — such as serving a mission for the Church, gaining a higher education, and pursuing further goals in athletics and schooling. These goals have kept me motivated yet have still allowed me freedom to do the other things I wanted to do.

"Important and helpful as these ideals and goals have been, some other ideals have been even more so despite their being in an area where understanding doesn't come easily.

6

As an example, I have always been able to relate to a basketball, for we know how each other thinks and will act. I can understand my school books, for they will always remain the same. But a few years ago I came in contact with a new element, an element which was very confusing and complicated — girls!

"Looking back to my dating experience from the beginning right up to the present, I am grateful that I established a second set of ideals dealing with this intriguing new topic. I first promised myself that I would never date a girl that I did not have the highest regard and respect for; that I would never place myself in a situation where extreme temptation could take place. In addition, I would always treat the girl I was dating as a young lady and try to display proper manners in her company. More than that, I would not downgrade any girl or girls in general (or myself!) by crude talk about them such as goes on in the locker room or in other gatherings of guys.

"I'm glad to say that I've lived up to these ideals. For all that, life still has given me a great deal of challenge and a good many problems to face. I'm told it never will be easy, and I can believe it, but I have found that by adhering to these ideals I can really enjoy life's experiences to the full. And since my short life has taught me that by holding fast to my ideals and goals I can enjoy more of the fun-producing and growth-producing activities and miss most of the discouraging and destructive ones, I think I'd be foolish if I didn't conclude that that's the way to go throughout life."

Well, there you have it — the good word from your own generation. Bear in mind that Karen and David are not geniuses — special people, yes, but every one of us is special because of our divine lineage. You have just as much opportunity to become the right one as any other of today's youth. In this book I want to share with you some ways in which you can do this, some ways in which you can more clearly understand your role as a son or daughter of God and a member of his true Church.

As you read, remember that you are not competing with anyone else. Like you, everyone else is a unique personality. By all means emulate good examples, but you have no right to feel discouraged because you are not like someone else. Let me share with you a brief thought I heard expressed several years ago and which I have adopted as a guideline in life: "There is no nobility in being superior to another person. True nobility is being superior to one's past self."

It is the reach for your better self that will make you the right one.

Chapter 2

Be You, Be True

In chapter 1 I made the somewhat unoriginal statement that everyone is a unique personality. Think about that for a moment. It means not only that you are not like anyone else but also that no one else is quite like you. Not so apparent but equally true, it means that in the genius of the Lord's plan each of us is gifted with certain native talents and endowments which, properly developed and used, will bring happiness to their possessor and benefit to those in his circle of influence. That, after all, is a major lesson of the parable of the talents.

LDS youth know this and more, as they consider their present lives and the future potentials. Perhaps the question most often posed by young people today is, "Why am I as I am?" Many modern voices cry out that the individual is not responsible for what he is, that he is simply the product of his environment. This absolutely is untrue. It runs entirely against the grain of our revealed religious beliefs. While it is true that undoubtedly we bring talents and tendencies with us from the preexistent life, it is also true that mortality is part of an eternity in which progress is the key to happiness, and that talents and trials, helps and handicaps are all part of our upward reach. Though everyone's vehicle is different, the road rules are the same for all. So is the desired destination — eternal life. No one is precluded from that goal because he is not the same as someone else.

Similarly, we are not slaves to environment, but instead are expected to act purposefully upon it. "God . . . hath created all things, both the heavens and the earth, and all things that in them are, both things to act and things to be acted upon." (2 Nephi 2:14.) As a child of God, you were created to act upon things and not be acted upon.

So the proper counsel to you is, Be you, be true. That is, recognize your uniqueness. Enjoy it. By all means develop the good characteristics that contribute to it. But always acknowledge completely the other side of the coin — your similarities to and brotherhood with every other child of God. Don't let an unreasoning pride in your uniqueness, or a carelessness about what that means for your future, drive you off the road into the ditch. Be you, yes, but be true too — true to your better self and to the long and straight road of progress which will lead all our dissimilar vehicles to that greatest of all destinations.

Since we each have our own peculiarities as well as our own potential, it becomes an endless endeavor for us to utilize the one in achieving the other. This necessitates that each of us seek to understand himself. One factor in this understanding is recognizing the close relationship between our physical condition, our thinking, and our feelings, since each of these three aspects influences and is influenced by the other two.

Let me give a personal example. When I was a small boy I spent one afternoon melting crayons in an old tin can over a fire in the backyard. As I picked up the can with a pair of pliers I tripped and fell, causing the boiling wax to spill all over my hands, arms, and stomach. As I cried out in pain with these third-degree burns I became irrational, and with tears in my eyes I told my parents that I really wanted to die.

10

Clearly, at that time both my mind and my emotions were virtually governed by my body, by my physical condition.

On the other hand, some have managed to develop such a mental and spiritual control over the body as even to conquer the effects of physical pain. Some of the early Christian martyrs must have been like that. So was Abinadi, the Book of Mormon prophet-martyr who was burned at the stake but who continued prophesying in the midst of the consuming flames.

This demonstrates that it is possible for each of us to learn to exercise proper control of his emotions and physical urges. So as you pass through these precious years of "becoming," be sure to impose upon yourselves a conscious standard of excellence that requires an "on guard" position, thereby controlling your body, your mind, and your emotions.

Even though, as we discussed earlier, an environment not of your choosing cannot control your life, a bad environment of your own selection has you at a disadvantage from the start. I was forcibly reminded of this fact not long ago when I met a young lady who under normal circumstances had diligently maintained the "on guard" position. In a moment of weakness, however, she found herself at a party where alcohol was being served. After several refusals she at length let down her mental and spiritual guard, submitted to the enticements of her friends by drinking, and finally left the party minus her virtue. The overwhelming sorrow and guilt she experienced when she realized what she had done, and that in addition to having violated the law of chastity she was now pregnant, cannot be expressed in words. She had fought a good fight every day of her life except one, and that one mistake tragically influenced the course of her life.

A negative experience such as I have just mentioned would take a lot of repenting to counteract. Positive experiences, on the other hand, leave no regrets and are builders

11

of character. Interestingly, you can't always know at the time just how much influence a given experience will have upon your life and character.

Let me give you an unusual type of example from the life of a modern Church leader — President Hugh B. Brown, who lived until 1975. In 1904, while not yet twenty-one, he was called on a mission to England. What influence would this have on his life and character? A great deal. For example, it was a basic training-ground for the development of his subsequent skills as an orator. But there was a more specific and direct result than that. Hugh Brown wanted to be a lawyer. And in those days this could sometimes be achieved by a type of apprenticeship or on-the-job training. But just about that time it was becoming general to require some preparatory college work preceding this apprenticeship, and Brother Brown had done none of this work. Read now what happened.

12

"Hugh wrote to the president of the University of Alberta about his varied experience, including his missionary work, and asked if an exception to the normal academic requirements for admission might be made. The reply was that he would need at least two more years of formal schooling to qualify. This was very discouraging to Hugh, who had limited means and could not afford to leave income-producing work again. For a time his career plans were derailed.

"Then a remarkable incident put his hopes back on the track. The Alberta Stake conference was being held in Cardston when the head of the University of Alberta happened to be in the little Mormon community en route to Waterton Lakes. He came to the meeting and was invited to sit on the stand. Recognizing the pulpit talent for which Hugh already had a local reputation, President Wood announced at the beginning of the meeting, 'We're going to ask Elder Hugh B. Brown to be the speaker today, as we have a number of distinguished visitors. Elder Brown has recently been on a mission to England and can represent the Church well.' Hugh, who had been home from his mission for six years, later recalled that he spoke on 'the first principles of the Gospel and the restoration thereof.' He then sat down by the university president, who turned to him and asked, 'Are you the Mr. Brown who wrote to me about joining the Law Society?' Hugh said, 'Yes, sir.' The educator continued, 'And I turned you down, didn't I?' 'You did,' was the answer. The president then said, 'If you will write me tomorrow morning, I'll change the verdict. No man can talk like you have done today and not be entitled to be a law student.' " (Eugene E. Campbell and Richard D. Poll, *Hugh B. Brown, His Life and Thought* [Salt Lake City: Bookcraft, 1975], pp. 76-77.)

When the young Hugh Brown was on his mission, and even when he stood up to talk in that stake conference, he could not have guesed at the far-reaching effects of the experience. Half a century later he observed, "That was the most profitable sermon I ever preached." It opened the way to achieving a major goal in his life, for he went on from there to become a lawyer as planned.

13

What President Brown displayed here was a constancy of purpose and action — he set his goal and worked steadfastly towards it, and the positive experiences of the past combined to help him achieve it.

Do you similarly recognize the importance of constancy in your actions? It is when a person develops constancy, the ability to move steadfastly in a purposeful direction, that his life becomes meaningful to himself and valuable to others. Lying in front of a television set every evening, wasting hours upon hours on the telephone, or reading shallow literature just to occupy the mind — all these "activities" help to develop a person into one big "nothing." The key is desire, desire to do something with life. Someone once said, "He who desireth nothing shall not be disappointed."

Remember again, in moving ahead you are not competing

with anyone else but only with your past self. In that effort you must make the best use you can of your positive experiences. Further, you ought to help others to have such experiences.

One young man came to see me who was deep in thought. He had not said two words in my seminary class, so I was quite surprised when he appeared at my door. As he sat down he began to cry. For five full minutes both of us sat in a silence broken only by sobs as his heart opened and released the host of feelings he had been harboring for a long time.

Finally regaining his composure, and taking a deep breath, he spoke, "Brother Yorgason, I have sat in your class for three weeks now, and never once have you called on me to participate."

I was stunned. Before I could respond, he continued.

"When I was in the fourth grade my teacher called me a dummy for something I said that was incorrect. From then on my friends nicknamed me 'Dummy.' As time passed, I began to believe that I was just what they said I was. Now I am seventeen, and I just can't go on feeling this way about myself. What can I do?"

Once again the worth of each person as an individual rang clearly in my mind. Many of you have experienced the pain of nonacceptance and have consequently "lived down" to your understanding of others' expectations of your behavior. This is another negative type of experience, and a common one. I was shocked to think that I had unconsciously helped to provide it for this young man, when supplying its opposite was my intent and my function. From this story you can see that even when a person desires to achieve, one small uncalled-for action by any one of us could throw the switch that alters that person's destination.

After reading this chapter you will recognize how important it is for you to grasp the positive experiences of your life.

Create them, even, for yourself and for others. In this way you can become, and help others to become, an adult who has the self-confidence and self-esteem we all need and ought to have.

And as you pursue this goal, in your objective and your actions recognize both your uniqueness and your similarity to other children of God. In other words, be you but be true.

Chapter 3

Entertaining the Emotions

Scene 1: Gary stood in the shadows as he watched Tonya, his girl friend, and Dave drive away from the game together. Once again the feelings of resentment and jealousy swelled inside. "David, my very best buddy, always butting in with every girl I start to go with. If only I had the guts, I would tell him just where to get off!" The problem: Gary doesn't have the guts.

Scene 2: Barbara stood stoically in line for her ticket to Chicago. For the third time in the past month she had proven to herself that she was not a winner. "I can't wait to get away and lose myself," she thought. "First I failed my interview to be in the university senate. Then I didn't get accepted into a sorority, and finally today I failed the orchestra audition. Oh, well, I didn't want to be in it anyway. I've just got to get away and forget it."

Scene 3: "Get off my back, Eileen! You and your churchy parents — all you ever do is connive and scheme against me! You're all just as phony as the rest of 'em!"

With that, Sam slammed the door, leaving Eileen shocked and in tears.

Scene 4: Harlan sat in meditation as the breeze filtered down through the quakies. "The first day of the hunt, and what a beautiful day it is," he thought to himself. "Sheri. Wow! She is really something else! I bet we would have had the sharpest time last night at homecoming. I've never really talked to her, but I bet we could really communicate. Maybe I should write her a letter when we get back to camp tonight. No, that would be too presumptuous. Hey, I bet when we bumped into each other in the hall Tuesday that she did it intentionally. You know, big fella, some day you really oughtta strike up a conversation with that lass. She'd be forever indebted."

Scene 5: As she finished brushing her hair Margaret felt a deep sense of urgency. Tonight she and Paul were driving all the way to Salt Lake City to attend the reception of his closest companion from the mission field. "Why, it hardly seems possible that Paul has been home from his mission for seven months now," she mused. "And to think we met that very week."

17

Suddenly her heart leaped as the doorbell rang. For some reason this night seemed more special than any other, and yet it hadn't even begun.

Following the reception, Paul and Margaret decided to dine at La Caille. "After all," thought Margaret, "wouldn't it be special to return to the place of our first date?"

The candle flickered with excitement as this young couple enjoyed the final bites of their cheesecake. Then, without warning, their eyes met — really for the first time. Knowing full well that she could contain herself no longer, Margaret blurted, "Paul, I — I — "

"I know," interrupted Paul, "and I love you, too!"

The dramatizations you have just read illustrate several alternative ways of handling emotions. In the first scene, Gary was unable to express his emotion to his best friend, so he chose to suppress it. This occurs all too frequently in our interactions with one another.

In scene two, Barbara's approach to handling her emotions was to divert her attention from that which was bothering her to something totally unrelated. Using diversion tactics can be beneficial or they can serve as scapegoat mechanisms, depending upon the situation.

The third scene made us witness to Sam, who impulsively expressed an emotion without any real care concerning the effects of his outburst. This is a common method of accommodating emotions, particularly for those who have not yet reached an acceptable level of emotional maturity.

In the next scene, we find Harlan dealing with his emotions for Sheri by constructing daydreams. This is a relatively harmless way to handle emotions; that is, unless it becomes such a habit that a person substitutes real expression of emotions for the daydreams. When this occurs, especially if it occurs repeatedly, the individual is using the daydreaming to escape from reality.

As scene five unfolds, we find a somewhat more pleasurable situation. Margaret and Paul have matured in their relationship. Because theirs has been an open and honest expression of feelings and values, they arrive at the moment in their lives when it becomes appropriate for both to express their love for each other.

These examples show that when an individual feels an emotion, he has certain alternative ways of handling or expressing this emotion. It is quite obvious that some methods of accommodating emotions are healthier and more appropriate than others. Wouldn't it be of value to now consider what emotions are, and how you can most appropriately adjust to the ones you have?

Emotions are much more than a set of impulses. You don't simply burst into tears or throw your hands into the

18

air in desperation without cause. Such outbursts merely display the consequences of existing conditions in your life.

Have you ever been made to feel guilty or ashamed because you possessed a particular emotion? This should not be so. In his book *Love and Marriage,* F. A. Magoun states: "No one need ever be ashamed of any honest emotion, no matter what it is. The emotion is only a consequence; the cause is the thing that is making trouble. Causes lie in the conditions which produce emotions. The problem of honestly recognizing our emotions is the most important single problem in preparing for a happy marriage . . . if indeed not in life, itself. Until an individual knows how he feels and why, he cannot know what he is or what he thinks." (F. A. Magoun, *Love and Marriage* [New York: Harper & Brothers, 1956], p. 84.)

Although it is imperative that you come to grips with your emotions; that is, develop an open and honest expression of these emotions, this is just the beginning. In order for a couple to develop a viable and satisfying marriage relationship, they must be open and honest with each other and with their emotions, but they must also develop an acceptable level of emotional maturity. While a person may be very candid and open in expressing his emotions, he may be expressing them in a damaging and totally unacceptable manner.

As an example, if a young man who goes to pick up his date has a chip on his shoulder because of the way he was treated in football practice, he may feel justified in shouting and verbally attacking his girl friend for no apparent reason. Yes, he is being open and honest in expressing how he feels, but he is performing in a very immature manner. As I approached the gymnasium to attend a basketball game not long ago, I rounded a corner and came face to face with two young people (they dated each other steadily) verbally battling it out. The girl had gone to the game with her girl friends because he was late in picking her up. Their problem

19

was magnified by the fact that he had not scored well on a test that day, and so he was giving it to her with both barrels.

Luckily these two young people are not married, since they obviously are not mature enough to handle the emotions they are experiencing. It is sad to think of all the marriages that end in divorce simply because one or both partners have not gained a tolerable level of emotional maturity.

Try to become sensitive to the conditions in your life which produce the emotions you have. If you find yourself repeatedly involved in relationships which do not provide a solid emotional base, perhaps you should step back and analyze the way in which you accommodate your emotions.

You should be relieved to know that you are not alone in your dilemma. Everyone who reaches emotional maturity must pass through growing and "groaning" experiences. Find hope in the fact that you are learning and overcoming, and that you are developing a solid foundation for your marriage.

Chapter 4

Give-and-Take Relationships

If it were possible to isolate the most rewarding and most universal desire of mankind (other than basic survival), it would undoubtedly be the desire to interact and relate well with others. Because we are basically social beings, those individuals who make an effort to relate and positively interact with others find a greater measure of fulfillment in their lives.

Beginning with day one, our lives are caught in the mainstream of survival, and we survive by maximizing our rewards and minimizing our punishments. As children, we learn the importance of relating to our parents, and then to our brothers and sisters. The result of these efforts is the building and establishing of meaningful relationships.

The types of relationships we establish vary greatly, although they begin with our immediate family unit, called our family of orientation. From this unit we explore other relationships, usually beginning with those of our own sex. Young people who are capable of developing a relationship at this level will be more likely to succeed in building relationships with those of the opposite sex. The culmination of developing relationships is, of course, the establishing of a new family unit, or a family of procreation. Since this is the goal of almost all young people, it would be well to explore how we interact with others, and thus determine how successful relationships are formed.

Although there are many types of relationships, they are all developed and maintained through social interaction. When two people meet for the first time, a wide range of behavior is possible between them. As the relationship develops, each partner learns to give and take in a manner acceptable to the other. You no doubt remember how uneasy and insecure you felt as you began to explore what was acceptable and what was not acceptable in a new relationship. Isn't it a relief when both of you begin to understand the boundaries you have set in your relationship? As the boundaries are set, a line is figuratively drawn by both of you. That line separates what is and what is not to transpire in your relationship.

22

As an example, not long ago a student with an obviously heavy heart came in to see me. She had been dating one of the most outgoing and popular guys on campus, and consequently was the envy of many other girls. She told me that everything was going well in their relationship until the previous Saturday night. They had spent the evening watching television in her home. Her parents were gone for the weekend, so they felt quite comfortable with each other. As the evening progressed, this girl was concerned that their making out would lead to doing things they would regret later. Even with a full awareness of what was about to happen, she left herself no margin of safety. Before she realized it, he was all over her with his hands. After petting for some time, she mustered up enough strength to pull herself away and run crying up to the kitchen. She then realized that although she had drawn a line for herself, her desire to please her boy friend had caused her to draw a lower line defining what was acceptable in their physical relationship.

The sad thing about this experience is that they jumped so quickly into the physical part of their relationship that they did not have time to define what was and what was not acceptable. Luckily they went no further, but they have each visited with their respective bishops, and are working on regaining their personal worthiness. Incidentally, they have decided that they abused the privilege of dating each other, so they have broken up.

As you consider the value of forming right relationships in your critical years, spend a little time with the following ideas. They represent my personal views and priorities in forming meaningful relationships:

1. The more interaction and communication I have with another person, the more confident I become in that relationship.

2. As I interact with others in forming relationships, I cling to those people who share similarities, and I tend to draw away from those persons who do not seem to have things in common with me.

3. When a person tells me something about himself, and then demonstrates behavior which is inconsistent with what he has said, I begin to lose respect for that person. I appreciate real people, don't you?

4. The more attentive I become toward other people, the more I feel a closeness with them as they respond to my attentiveness.

5. The more I interact with other people, the more I find that there are some people for whom I have special affinity. They are the ones who supply me with fulfillment and satisfaction in my life.

6. The more honest and open I am about myself with another person, the more meaningful my relationship with that person becomes. This introduces the element of trust, which is essential in developing and maintaining meaningful relationships.

7. The more a person confides and trusts in me, the more I reciprocate by placing trust in that person.

23

8. The more a person confides and places trust in me, the harder I strive to maintain that trust placed in me.

9. The more I am willing to give of myself in my interaction with another person, the more I find myself recipient of intrinsic rewards from my interaction with that person. In other words, I am a reward-seeking, punishment-avoiding creature, and so by giving, I receive. Edwin Markham, a noted literary artist, once said:

> There is a destiny that makes us brothers;
> None goes his way alone.
> All that we send into the lives of others
> Comes back into our own.

10. I have also discovered that I am a strong-willed person, and so in developing a relationship, if I sense that another person is trying to take advantage of me, I will quickly withdraw from that relationship.

25

Although these ideas are not conclusive, they encompass the major factors that my experience tells me should be considered in seeking to establish meaningful relationships.

Why not make it your personal goal to upgrade your own personality so that you will become the type of person with whom others will desire to associate?

Chapter 5

More Than Small Talk

That first date with someone can tend to be an unsettling experience. What is really going on in the mind of the other person? In the first part of this chapter I reproduce the words of an author I have been unable to identify, as he represents the feelings and mutual misinterpretations possible on such a date.

Seen through the eyes of Bonnie Armstrong

I was nervously taking a last-minute look at myself in the mirror when the doorbell rang, and when it did, about eight thousand butterflies took wing in my stomach. I had waited a whole year for this night. I had thought Mark Padderson was never going to take the hint and ask me out. And if this evening didn't turn out to be perfect, I knew he'd never ask me again.

With that discomforting thought in mind, I tried to quiet my knocking knees and open the door.

Mark stood on the front doorstep, the porch light blazing down on the gorgeous dark hair every girl in school would love to run her fingers through.

He smiled. "Hi, you look nice."

I didn't look nice at all. My hair hadn't turned out, and the really sharp dress I'd wanted to wear was at the cleaners.

I smiled back anyway. "Thanks, so do you," I said, and immediately wished I hadn't. How dumb can you get? You just don't say that kind of thing to a boy — even when he does look nice.

When we were settled in his car, Mark turned to me, "Where would you like to go?"

Something in the area of my midsection dropped ten feet. That wasn't fair! How did I know where he could afford to go? And how dull he's going to think I am if I don't suggest something exciting.

"Wherever you want to go," I said, chalking up the second point against me. I was in rare form tonight. I'd managed to be both dumb and dull in less than two minutes. And, I had a feeling this was only the beginning.

Mark looked and smiled again — or pretended to, anyway.

"How about going to the Capitol?"

Then something dropped ten more feet. The Capitol was a nearby movie theater.

"I've seen the picture," I said miserably. Bonnie Armstrong, girl failure.

Mark thought a moment. "How about the Starlight?"

I coughed violently. The Starlight was a drive-in theater. No drive-ins for me. That was kind of a rule my friends and I had. "I've seen that picture, too," I lied, wondering what was playing and praying he wouldn't ask. I also wished I were dead.

Mark looked as if he was going to laugh, but he didn't.

"What movie haven't you seen?"

"The one at the Lyric," I said weakly. I'd seen that one too, but at this moment I wouldn't have admitted it under oath.

This time Mark did laugh, right out loud. In fact, he laughed several times on the way to the Lyric, and I chalked up several more points against me.

27

Nothing disastrous happened between the parking lot and the lobby, and I was beginning to relax when he walked over to the refreshment stand.

Mark gave me a questioning look. Assuming that he was asking if I wanted something, I shook my head no.

Then he ordered two boxes of popcorn and promptly handed me one. He'd mistaken my nod to mean yes, and somehow that figured. What difference did it make that I despised popcorn? It gave me the world's noisiest hiccups every time I even looked at it! Nothing had gone right yet, so why should it start now?

The movie (which, by the way, I hadn't seen once — I'd seen it twice) was about one-fourth over when I realized Mark wasn't watching the movie. He was watching me. That figured, too. There I was, gazing vacantly at the screen, clutching the unopened box of popcorn like it was an old friend.

"Don't you want your popcorn?" he asked when our eyes met.

"Of course," I blurted, much too loudly.

Someone behind us said, "Shut up!" in a very impolite tone of voice.

Returning my vacant gaze to the screen, I bravely opened the box of popcorn. I ate one kernel, and held my breath. Nothing happened. I ate another kernel. Then several things happened. First, I hiccuped so resoundingly that it was heard all over the theater. Second, although I'd been expecting it to happen, the hiccup startled me so much that the entire box of popcorn spilled all over Mark's lap. Last, but hardly least, I started to laugh. I tried not to but I just couldn't help it. Then that aforementioned someone behind us told us to shut up this time or else. I did.

Solemnly but silently swearing never to open my ridiculous mouth again as long as I lived, I watched the remainder of the movie without seeing it. All through it I was conscious,

28

too conscious, of Mark beside me. How I loved the thought of his being there, and the knowledge that he'd never be there again made me want to start bawling. Considering my track record for the evening, it's a wonder I didn't go right ahead and bawl.

After the movie we went to a drive-in restaurant. It was then that I began to wonder what I'd ever done to deserve all this.

Mark ordered a hamburger *with* onions!

The waitress looked at me; I looked back at the waitress. She looked back at me. "Well?" she said at last, and not too kindly.

Well what? If I didn't order a hamburger, Mark was going to think I didn't want to kiss him goodnight. I wasn't going to kiss him anyway (another of those rules), but I didn't want to give him the idea I wanted him to kiss me (which I did), but wouldn't, if you know what I mean.

I sighed wholeheartedly. "I'll have a hamburger without." And I'll be darned if Mark didn't laugh again. My face flamed, and when the hamburger arrived, I bit into mine like I expected it to bite me back.

When the waitress came back to pick up the tray, Mark looked at his watch. "Hey, it's after eleven!" he said, and sounded worried. "I've got to get home. I have basketball in the morning."

I made myself nod politely. Basketball practice, my eye! On Saturday? Precisely who was he trying to kid? Me, that's who. I even knew what would come next. We'd drive home and he would walk me to the door. He'd say it had been fun and that he'd call me. And he never would. That was perfectly all right with me because I wouldn't come to the phone anyway. Future conversations were out of the question!

We drove home; Mark walked me to the door. "It's been fun," he said. "I'll call you," he added.

29

And then, instead of trying to kiss me good-night, or asking if he could, he simply reached up and patted me on the head. Patted me! I fully expected him to say, "Good-night, Rover," but he didn't. He just said good-night and sprinted back to the car.

When I got up to my room I thought about Mark and our date. What a disaster!

I wound my hair spitefully on the most uncomfortable rollers I owned, and went to bed feeling that I wouldn't be able to sleep a wink.

I fell asleep immediately, hoping morning would never come.

Seen through the eyes of Mark Padderson

30

I must have stood on the Armstrong doorstep for at least five full minutes before I rang the bell. For some crazy reason, I suddenly didn't want to go out with Bonnie.

It wasn't because Bonnie wasn't cute or popular; she was that and a lot more. I guess it was because I knew it was going to be like all the other dates I went on.

You see, athough I don't really know why, the girls around school consider me some kind of a catch or something. As far as I can see, about the only thing that makes me any different from the rest of the guys is that I'm available. I've never gone steady in my life! And you know what that does to a girl.

I didn't have to wonder if Bonnie was going to act just like the other girls who had tried to snare me. I knew. She had sort of a thing for me, and had had it for a long time. Now that I had asked her out for a date, I knew what was in store for me.

For the next four hours, Bonnie was going to do everything she could to make sure her hook got into me but solid.

She was going to be perfect. She'd look perfect, act perfect, and try everything in her power to give me the "ten feet tall" feeling that some girls have the mistaken idea they're capable of giving.

Tonight she'd be an alluring, willing slave to the poor defenseless male she hoped to master. Unfortunately, that poor defenseless male was me.

But, what the heck. I rang the doorbell anyway.

I must say that when she answered the door, I immediately knew I'd been right about one thing. She did look perfect. Her hair was soft and natural instead of piled up like a haystack. Instead of the usual too-fancy dress, she was wearing a black skirt and a red sweater. As I said, she looked perfect.

I smiled. "Hi," I said. "You look nice."

She smiled back. "Thanks, so do you."

So do you? That was a funny thing for a girl to say. They usually expect you to spend about two years getting all shaved and dressed up for them, but you're the one who has to dish out the compliments.

When we settled down in the car, I had every intention of starting and heading for the Lyric. It was playing the only movie I hadn't seen, but I just couldn't resist asking a question I already knew the answer to.

Turning to her, I said, "Where would you like to go?"

She would, of course, have a list of exciting places to mention so I'd think she was about the sharpest girl alive.

"Wherever you want to go," she replied.

That was a surprise! But I knew she'd rise to the bait on the next question.

"How about going to the Capitol?" I knew she'd seen that movie because I'd seen her there two nights before. But she'd never admit to it on a bet. It wouldn't be the perfect thing to do.

31

"I've seen the picture," Bonnie said at last.

"Okay," I thought, "have it your way. Don't try to be perfect. Try to be different. That's a good form of attraction, too." Now, what would a girl who is trying to be different do to prove it?

"How about the Starlight?" I asked, which was a stroke of sheer genius. Most of the girls had some silly rule about no drive-ins on dates, but not when they're trying to be different.

Bonnie caught her breath and coughed as if she had just swallowed the answer to my question. "I've seen that picture, too," she lied hopefully. I don't know why I knew she was lying — I just did — and all of a sudden I felt like laughing.

"What movie haven't you seen?" I asked, knowing she wouldn't say the Lyric because that's where I wanted to go.

She looked very perplexed for a second (this kid must go to an awful lot of movies), and then she spoke. "The one at the Lyric."

I don't know why that made me feel like laughing again, but this time I couldn't keep from doing it. It must have been that odd look on her face or something. And every time I thought about it on the way to the Lyric, I laughed some more. She didn't say anything. She just sort of looked like she was counting something in her head. Probably totaling up the number of movies she'd been to this week.

When we reached the lobby, I asked her if she wanted something, and she waved her head around a couple of times. Rather than go through the trouble of figuring out whether she meant yes or no, I bought her a box of popcorn and let it go at that.

The movie was about one-fourth of the way through when I had the sudden urge to look over at her. She was staring at the screen with that glassy-eyed look people get when they're watching a television re-run for the three-thousandth time. And she was clutching her unopened box of popcorn like it was an old friend.

I figured the glassy-eyed look out right away. The little devil had seen the movie before, but then, at the rate she went to the movies, how could she have helped it? But the popcorn-clutching bit — that I didn't get.

"Don't you want your popcorn?" I asked, figuring I'd eat it if she didn't.

"Of course," she blurted, in the loudest whisper I think I've ever heard, and opened the popcorn box as though she thought it had a bomb in it. Then she started eating popcorn, holding her breath, then eating more popcorn and holding her breath some more. I was about to ask her what in the something-or-other she was up to when she practically rocked the theater with the biggest, loudest hiccup in history. And that's not all. It scared her so much that she jumped and the whole box of popcorn landed all over my lap.

33

Instead of running out of the theater or crawling under her seat from embarrassment, she did the craziest thing. She burst out laughing! I wanted to join her, but some guy behind us started complaining. After that hiccup, he sort of had a point, too.

I have to admit that I watched the rest of the movie without really seeing it. Boy, if this wasn't the weirdest date I'd ever been on in my life.

On the way home from the movie I dared to make a last attempt. This girl had to do something normal. The law of averages proved that. So I drove into the Burger-Inn and dropped the bomb.

I ordered a hamburger *with*. The minute I did it I felt sorry. That's just about the dirtiest trick a guy can pull on a first date. It completely wipes the girl out. She doesn't know what to do. If she orders the same, she thinks the boy thinks she wants him to kiss her good-night, which she does, but she won't let him if he tries. On the other hand, if she orders a hamburger without, she thinks the boy is going to think she doesn't want to kiss him, and she doesn't want that to happen either. (I often wonder about girls, don't you?)

Every time I've pulled this on a girl, she's risen above the whole matter and solved everything by ordering a root beer. I waited for Bonnie to do just that.

It's a good thing I didn't hold my breath waiting, because after the waitress prompted Bonnie a little, she said, "I'll have a hamburger *without*." And the way she emphasized *without* just about cracked me up. She got all red, and all of a sudden I felt sorry for her, so I shut up.

Then I remembered about tomorrow. I had a basketball practice at 9:00 A.M. That coach really had a heart, but I suppose with such a big game coming up, he wasn't taking any chances.

34

"Hey," I said, looking at my watch, "it's after eleven. I've got to go home. I have a basketball practice in the morning."

Bonnie's reaction really took the cake.

You know how girls get when they think you've given them the business. They give you this big "I couldn't care less" look, and act like they can hardly wait to get rid of you.

Bonnie made an attempt to wave her head around, but her eyes looked like a couple of stones. She not only felt unhappy, but she was madder than you know what. She plain didn't believe me, and it showed. It was about the most honest reaction I've ever seen a girl have.

I wanted to say something else, but since I couldn't think of anything, I kept quiet until we got to her house. At the door, I knew what I wanted to say, yet I couldn't say it.

Something really crummy was happening to me. I was flipping over this girl. She was so cute and so screwy, and her hooks were into me but good.

"It's been fun," I said after we had stood on the doorstep looking at each other for what seemed like a week. That was a pretty stupid thing to say, I know, but what was I supposed to say? I love you? If I did that, she would probably get the hiccups again and wake up the whole neighborhood. Besides, I didn't. Or did I? Oh, well, who knows about stuff like that, anyway?

She didn't say anything at all, but she smiled at me sort of strangely. "I'll call you," I continued. I wanted to kiss her so much I could taste it. But I could also taste those darn onions, so I decided against it.

Instead, I reached up and touched her hair. It came out more like a pat on the head, but it was better than nothing.

With that, I knew I'd better get out of here or I would be coming on strong, onions or no onions. I practically sprinted back to the car.

All the way home I wondered when to call her. I felt like calling her that night, but no girl is going to wind me around her little finger! I'd wait and call her in the morning before I went to basketball practice. Sure, it'd be pretty early, but she was one girl who didn't need her beauty sleep. And how!

When I got home, I chewed a couple of pieces of gum so I could stand to be in the same room with myself and those stupid onions. Then I crawled into bed, knowing I was too keyed up to sleep a wink. Imagine me, ol' Mark Padderson, trapped! Just the thought of it was enough to scare a guy awake for the next eleven years.

I fell asleep immediately, wishing morning would hurry up.

35

Can You Communicate?

As you can see from this example, the first date can seem like a total disaster! Many of you repeat this experience again and again, never knowing exactly how it can be circumvented.

As you have no doubt guessed, lack of communication is not limited to the first date. Many couples struggle and squirm through months of similar experiences simply because they have not learned the skills of positive communication.

Learning to communicate is perhaps the most essential tool in building successful and lasting relationships. It does not occur without a great deal of effort, regardless of the persons involved. Nor can you limp through a rocky home life until age sixteen, then expect total success as you communicate with potential dating partners. Learning to communicate begins at birth, and young people who have the knack of getting along with anyone are those who have learned to give and take in the home with parents, with brothers and sisters, and with a significant number of others outside the home.

Before going further, perhaps we should define communication. Basically, it means to impart, to convey, or to make known. Communication involves an interchange of thoughts, opinions and facts, as well as feelings.

In order for communication to take place, there must exist a *sender,* a *receiver,* and a *message.* Each of these three is necessary for communication to transpire. For example, a person may expound on the deepest problems of his love life to the trees in a forest, yet he is not communicating because there is no receiver. When two people fight and shout at each other, they are both sending messages but neither is receiving, so discommunication takes place. There is never *no* communication when two people are interacting with each other. It is either communication or discommunication.

There are two forms of communication — verbal and nonverbal. Verbal communication involves using words in speaking or in writing. Speaking is the more accurate and satisfying of the two, as misunderstandings often develop when we communicate through writing. Have you ever written to your dating partner and expressed feelings you may have had regarding your relationship? And have you ever said something in the letter that was misinterpreted by your partner? Chances are that it took a phone call or face-to-face contact to clear up the misunderstanding. Even so, writing letters can provide an opportunity to express feelings on a very deep level. My wife and I were married for only eight months before I was sent to Viet Nam. The year we spent apart provided an opportunity for us to learn to communicate through letters, and we now have a lasting record of our thoughts, our feelings, and our experiences. We were able to discover each other in an exciting and unique way!

The second type of communication — nonverbal — is not as easily understood. There are many nonverbal ways to communicate, such as with facial expressions, vocal tones (which may completely change the meaning of that which is being said verbally), gestures with various parts of the body, touching, odor (positive, as with perfume or cologne, or negative, as with body odor or bad breath), mental or physical tensions, and body positions.

37

It is an interesting fact that only 10-20 percent of all communication is verbal, yet verbal communication is more easily understood. Because words have definite meanings, verbal communication is more accurate. Problems may arise, however, when words have several meanings. As an example, on my first date with my wife-to-be, I told her that I sold diamonds on a part-time basis to finance my schooling. At the end of the date, I said to her, "Maybe I'll give you a ring in a day or two." To me the "ring" meant a phone call, but she recalled our earlier conversation and thought I was extremely forward to think that I could give her an engagement ring after knowing her for only three days! Words *can* have many meanings.

The primary handicap in communicating nonverbally is that it can be easily denied. Suppose you really want to attract a girl's attention, so you sit opposite her in a cafeteria.

You may smile at her all through the meal, and though she knows exactly what you are doing (they usually do!), she may give you the "brush-off" by simply ignoring the signals you are giving. Or suppose you have taken a girl out several times, and on this particular night you feel that your relationship has progressed to the point that you want to give your date a good-night kiss. Upon reaching the front porch you thank her for the evening. She returns the thanks, at which time you close your eyes, bend down, turn your head slightly — waiting — waiting. Finally your eyes open just slightly, enough to see her bending down to pick up the evening paper. She knew exactly what you had in mind, yet your message was nonverbal, so she was able to deny having received it.

"Honest-to-goodness deep communication is essential." (K. L. Cannon, *Developing a Marriage Relationship* [Provo: Brigham Young University Publications, 1972], p. 48.) When we communicate, we gain a feeling of fulfillment of our needs. A person also gains recognition by communicating. This is something that we all desire, as we seek personal self-worth through being recognized for what we are and what we say.

In addition, communication permits a release of tensions. A major problem that couples may bring upon themselves after being married for a length of time is to let their emotions build up inside until they reach the bursting point. When this happens on a regular basis, discontentment with the relationship results. This occurs because most people are unable to limit an outburst to the situation at hand, and instead may wound their partner by becoming personal in their criticism. Releasing tensions can be a positive way of dealing with each passing experience.

Deciding that you can get away without communicating is a fallacy that you cannot afford to nurture. Always keep in mind that your partner has the same needs that you have; that is, to feel wanted, needed, valued, and loved.

Communication Obstacles

As we learn to communicate, there are several obstacles which need to be weeded out of our communication habits if we desire successful and rewarding relationships. In his book *Developing a Marriage Relationship,* K. L. Cannon deals with this thought in the following way.

First, the messages we may be sending to another do not always represent our true feelings. This is called masking. Perhaps we want to show our best side as we represent our ideas, or for another reason we may mislead the receiver. Suppose a young lady senses that her feelings toward her boy friend have changed, and she likes someone else. She may also realize that the prom is coming up in a week, and because she hasn't been able to communicate her feelings toward the new boy friend, she masks her change in feelings in communicating with the old boy friend so she will have a date. This type of masking is emotionally dishonest and immature.

There are times when we get so caught up in our own thoughts and ideas that we block out the other person's point of view completely. One of the most essential tools in communication is being able to place ourselves in the shoes of our partner, and see the situation from his point of view.

A lack of communication skills is another obstacle to be overcome. Sometimes we fall short of putting a message across because we lack the skill to convey the feelings or the emotions we have. Related to this is the idea that we sometimes experience a language inadequacy.

We may find it difficult to communicate our real feelings, so we merely communicate our reaction to these feelings. It is a skill to be able to differentiate between the two. For example, a dating relationship may become more serious than one of the partners considers healthy (in this instance, the boy). Because he feels inadequate in expressing his feelings about dating others, he simply begins dating other

girls without a word of explanation to his present girl friend. By not expressing his true feelings, he nonverbally expresses his reaction to his feelings. This unexpected turn of events causes the girl to phone him and, in an emotional outburst, say, "Why don't you love me anymore?" Now she is communicating her reaction to her feelings. Deep down inside she also feels that they are too serious, and that they must lighten up their relationship.

Situations arise which may cause one or both partners in a relationship to be afraid of the others' reaction and emotion, hence they postpone the inevitable — expressing how they really feel.

An additional obstacle in forming sound communication habits is the "double bind" communication. This arises when a partner expresses a feeling that places the receiver in a situation where he cannot resist, yet he cannot give in.

41

Perhaps an example will help to make this a little easier to understand. Kathy and Don have been dating for some time, and both very much desire to continue their relationship. Don has not been active in the Church, so he hasn't considered a mission in his future plans. Kathy, on the other hand, has promised herself for years that she would only marry a returned missionary.

One Saturday evening after a movie, Kathy turns to Don and says: "Don, I want you to know that I consider you the leader in our relationship. I respect your feelings and I want you to be the leader in our home. You are so understanding and honest, and are especially capable of making decisions for our good."

The conversation lags just a bit as the light from an oncoming car shines in their eyes. As the car passes, Kathy turns to Don and blurts out, "You've got to go on a mission, Don! You've got to honor your priesthood!"

At this point, Don cannot understand the feelings he is having. Thoughtfully he stews, asking himself: "What can

I say? First she says I am the leader in our relationship and that I am capable of making the right decisions, and then she says I have to go on a mission. If she truly believed that I could make the decision on my own because I hold the priesthood, why did she say that I have to go? If I tell her I'll go on a mission, then I'm knuckling to her. She'll be wearing the pants and making decisions for me. If I tell her I won't go, I am not honoring the priesthood like she says."

In this predicament, Don was left with a lose or lose alternative. He was hung regardless of how he answered. It's just like a wife awaking on Sunday morning, placing her foot on her husband's back, and saying as she pushes: "Jerry, you hold the priesthood and wear the pants in this family. Now get up and go to priesthood meeting!" I'm sure that you see the double bind surfacing.

42   Closely related to the double bind is the obstacle which arises when one partner fears hurting the other and so forestalls communicating the real feelings that are present.

Not long ago a friend of mine was preparing to get married in the temple. All of the final preparations for the reception were made, so there was a great deal of social pressure exerted on the couple to go through with their plans. Because her family opposed the marriage for various reasons, the girl felt more determined than ever to go through with it just to show her family that she knew what she was doing. Her other reason for wanting to go through with the marriage (by the way, she knew she did not love this particular young man) was because she feared the irrational behavior her fiance might exhibit if she was to back out. Fear of hurting her fiance's feelings nearly caused this young lady an eternity of misery. As it happened, about twelve hours before the ceremony was to take place she announced that she had changed her mind. She finally realized that with the stakes so high she could not play games, but that she had to honestly express and communicate the feelings she had.

Incidentally, this young lady grew ten feet tall in the eyes of her family that evening. They didn't think her "flaky" because of her actions. To the contrary, they knew that she would be forever grateful for having the maturity and fortitude to act on her convictions. This young lady is now happily married to the right person, is very much in love, and is rearing a beautiful family.

An additional situation which interferes with good communication is when one partner decides to damage the image of himself held by the other. This can be seen when a young man is jealous of his girl friend's feelings for others. Rather than talk his feelings out, he decides to get drunk and be seen with friends of questionable character.

In some instances it is inappropriate to discuss certain things. Several years ago I had the opportunity of reopening the island of Puerto Rico to missionary work. It was fascinating to learn the customs of that people, and to compare them with ours. Among the customs of the conventional Puerto Rican family is one forbidding teenagers from discussing with their dating partner any matters pertaining to sex. This seems strange to us, especially when two people are preparing for marriage. In our culture we encourage an open and mature exchange of ideas and emotions prior to marriage.

43

Perhaps the most critical obstacle to communicating is the habit that is built up over the years to simply not communicate. Many marriages disintegrate when one or both partners become aware that they cannot openly exchange feelings and emotions. This type of relationship is apparent in the case of a man coming home from work, slouching down in a chair, and spending night after night in front of the television set. The wife in turn is too busy to spend time with her husband, so theirs is a downward spiraling relationship that is doomed unless corrective action is taken. In your dating relationships, if your partner wants only to go to movies or watch television, this could be a signal for caution. As you prepare for marriage, make sure you select a mate who is desirous and capable of communicating. (Cannon, *Developing a Marriage Relationship,* pp. 43-47.)

Rules of Good Communication

In the story of *Alice in Wonderland,* Alice meets a clock with hands, arms, a face, etc. In the course of their conversation, Alice asks the clock what it is searching for in life. The clock responds that it is looking for the key that unlocks itself. Similarly, effective communication is the key which unlocks a relationship so that a couple can truly find themselves in each other.

Someone once wrote:

> 'Twixt optimist and pessimist
> The difference is droll.
> The optimist sees the doughnut;
> The pessimist, the hole.

Would you like to find the doughnut in your relationships; that is, those truths which lead to positive communication?

B. Rice suggested the following five rules for good communication:

1. State clearly and honestly what you feel. Be emotionally honest.
2. In both yourself and those with whom you are communicating, learn to recognize feelings which hinder communication — tiredness, frustration, and so on.
3. Make the whats, whys, and wherefores clear. Do you debate rather than discuss essential experiences you are having?
4. Listen to yourself. What communication tendencies do you have?
5. Assist others in learning to express their feelings.
   (B. Rice, CDFR 360 Class Lecture [Provo: Brigham Young University, 1970], p. 7.)

44

Remember that a person with good communication skills is a person who has warm, loving, empathetic feelings. Such a person is honest, open, trusting. But if you find yourself struggling and experiencing frustrations in your relationships with others, you are very normal. More important than the feelings you have is what you do about those feelings once you recognize them. Never allow your emotions to run away with your words. Instruct yourself that in anticipation of moments of crisis you should attack the situation rather than the person. If you do this, your partner will not be damaged by a personal attack.

A celestial marriage is one in which love, harmony, and understanding exist. I know that it is possible to *never* discredit your partner as you are resolving a conflict.

Yes, open and mature communication is a vital cog in the wheel of marriage. Reflect on the things that are discussed in this chapter. They can be of great value to you after marriage as well as before.

Chapter 6

Dating: Delights and Dilemmas

Did you know that very few of your grandparents, and virtually none of your great-grandparents participated in dating? It is a fairly new American custom, emerging in the 1920s. It may be difficult for you to comprehend that people marry without the dating experience, but this is the way it has been for thousands of years. Prior to relatively modern dating customs, couples were paired off by others, usually their parents. In fact, this is still done in many parts of the world.

By the mid-1900s dating was a well-established pattern of activity across the United States. Although you have grown up with the term *dating* being used as freely as the word *soapsuds*, still it might be interesting to define the term. Dating is a paired association between members of the opposite sex for a preplanned activity. It is "a social engagement of two young people with no commitment beyond the expectation that it will be a pleasurable event for both." (Burgess and Locke, *The Family: From Institution to Companionship* [New York, 1953], p. 331.)

Although you may wince at the description that a date is expected to be pleasurable for both partners (you've undoubtedly experienced the sheer agony of a poor date), there are several reasons why you keep going back for more. First, you date because you want to have fun and enjoy social experiences. Occasionally a date may "bomb," but more often than not this experience is forgotten as your head hits the pillow, and you begin dreaming of your next date.

As your dating experiences unfold, personal development occurs. This benefit of dating is not often thought of by you, but it is, in fact, one of the primary reasons your parents encourage you to date. Personal growth can occur as you make mistakes, then as you suffer and make amends for what you have said or done, and finally as you apologize and learn from what has happened. How many times have you said something like this: "Boy, I sure blew it! He'll never talk to me again. I'll never be dumb enough to do that again." Does that sound familiar?

As your relationships mature, you will find that you begin dating only the type of person who is a potential marriage partner. This occurs when you are tired of the "dating game," and you will then date primarily to select a marriage partner.

Although we usually like to talk only about the benefits of dating, there are also certain negative aspects that you know about. One of the greatest problems related to dating is *not* dating. Many young people develop severe inferiority complexes when they do not date. This obviously takes place more frequently with young ladies, since custom dictates that young men do most of the asking. There can be many obstacles to dating, some of them easily overcome.

Not long ago, a student came into my office, extremely depressed. After gathering up strength to speak, she finally blurted: "Why don't I ever date? I don't think I'm really bad-looking, yet I haven't had one date in my entire high school career!"

I seriously considered skirting the issue for fear of hurting her ego even more; then I decided my relationship with her was secondary to her growth and feelings of personal self-worth. I told her that during the two years I had known her, I had never seen her wear a dress. Her hair was unkempt,

and she wore no makeup. I suggested that she would begin to be treated like a young lady when she began to look and act like one. At first she pouted and explained away her appearance, but after a few moments she resolved to become more feminine in appearance. Would you believe that only weeks later she was asked out? She won!

It is true that personal appearance is not the only cause of young people not dating, but it can become a factor.

An additional problem of not dating is the "rating-dating" complex. This idea holds that young men date the young ladies who rate within their own peer group, and those who do rate are those who are successful in dating experiences. Some young ladies may rate too low for the majority of the boys, yet others may rate too high. If a girl rates too high, she may scare off potential dating partners, especially during her high school years.

49

If the "rating-dating" idea is correct, it would be a worthwhile ambition for young women to become attractive to young men by working to realize their potential. This might include improvement in grooming and dress, and developing talents. In other words, becoming the right one.

An additional cost of dating may be that it can impair personal growth and development. This happens when one or both partners place emphasis on appearance, superficial social skills, and small talk, and don't allow themselves to develop deep and meaningful communication with their dating partner.

As long as you use "fronts" rather than developing your real self, you are limiting, if not damaging, your personal growth. If you concentrate on important values and interests, gradually you will wean yourself away from playing the game.

One of the most difficult aspects of dating is the set of roles that both young men and young ladies identify as being proper in various dating situations. Especially are young ladies concerned, since one mistake may mean the end of a relationship. One of my students who was vitally concerned with this wrote the following poem.

WE CAN'T WIN

If a girl speaks to a boy, she's forward;
If she doesn't, she's bashful.
If she talks to a boy, she's a flirt;
If she doesn't, she's shy.
If she's smart in school, she's a sissy;
If she isn't, she's dumb.
If she talks about others, she's catty;
If she doesn't, she doesn't get along with others.
If she goes out with many boys, she's a pick-up;
If she doesn't, she's a wallflower.
If she's popular, she becomes an item of gossip;
If she isn't, she's ignored.
If she wears a boy's ring, she stole it;
If she doesn't, she couldn't get one.
If she tints her hair, she's cheap;
If she doesn't, she's chicken.
If she dances with underclassmen, she's robbin' the cradle;
If she doesn't, she has no school spirit.

— *Barbara Horton*

50

As you know, to define acceptable patterns of behavior is no easy task. If you want to know what type of person you are, or how you come across to your partner on a date, answer the following questionnaire.

Girls: Answer for yourselves
Boys: Answer the way you want a girl to answer
(Please answer *Yes* or *No*)

1. Do you like to always be in control on a date?
2. Do you rejoice when your date rejoices?
3. Do you wish to marry only a potentially successful person?

4. Do you enjoy being near your date?
5. Do you prefer being independent or not having to depend upon your date?
6. Do you admire your date?
7. Do you often reprimand your date for misbehavior?
8. Do you want to be tenderly cared for by your date?
9. Are you cautious on dates?
10. Do you dress to suit your date?
11. Do you stay at least one step ahead of your date?
12. Are you disturbed if your date is disturbed at you?
13. Do you wish you could stay at least one step ahead of your date?
14. Do you allow your date to make the decisions on the dates?
15. Do you subtly manipulate your date?
16. Do you accept your date's criticisms?
17. Do you try to make all the decisions on dates?
18. Would you ever go stag to a party?

51

You will be interested to know that you have just identified yourself (if you are a girl) as being either assertive or receptive. If you are a boy, you have just expressed your preference for dating an assertive or a receptive girl. Here's the definition of each of these two personality types.

Assertive. A person who is achievement-oriented, who dominates, who can be quite hostile, who is a status aspirant, or a status driver. An assertive person is one who takes the initiative or acts as an aggressor in most dating activities.

Receptive. A person who is deferential (enjoys caring for her date), who is prone to vicariousness (lives in a dream world), who is a hero worshipper, and one who is responsive in most dating activities to male initiative.

Now return to the questions. Add up all of the even-numbered questions you answered with a yes, and add up all of the odd questions you answered with a yes. Responding with a yes to most of the odd-numbered questions indicates that you are assertive if you are a girl, or that you prefer an assertive companion if you are a boy. On the other hand, if the majority of the yeses fall on the even-numbered questions, you are receptive, or you prefer dating girls who have a receptive nature. This exercise should enable you to learn a little more about your own personality, as well as what you desire in dating relationships.

Dating Values

Like most forms of social interaction, dating is a learned behavior. You actually begin learning how to date much earlier than your first dating experience, since you learn dating rules from parents, older brothers and sisters, others in your own peer group, and from the mass media.

Since dating is an investment of money, time, and personal talents and capabilities, it should have some value and rewards. Dates should be a meaningful venture in personal relationships between a boy and a girl. On a date you can plan on having a good time regardless of what you are doing if both of you share the responsibility of making the evening enjoyable and your relationship at least respectful. Too often, one partner or both have a miserable experience simply because they transfer the responsibility of having a good experience to the other person. This same person often shifts the blame for an unpleasant date onto the shoulders of his dating partner.

You will come to appreciate that many of those you date eventually become your lifelong friends. As you grow in your dating relationships, you will find a bond developing between you and your partner. This is not an unbreakable trust, but it is a significant feeling of confidence. Then, as your dating becomes more frequent and you begin to share values, it becomes easier for your relationship to encompass other expressions of trust and security.

Dating can also be a special way of getting to know and understand yourself as well as your dating partners. I think it is exciting to realize that dating allows you the opportunity to broaden and deepen your perspectives.

One of the basic needs which dating satisfies for you is that of group status. I remember that it was vitally important for me to know that I had status within my group, and this was achieved with my dating experiences. Have you ever considered that dating is actually a group activity, even though the interaction occurs between you and your partner? This is true because you must abide by the rules set by your group if you wish to retain status in your group.

Because you achieve group status by functioning according to the expectations of your group, dating gives you personal assurance. I am sure that you know many of your peers who feel either unworthy, unwanted, or unattractive. Dating counteracts these feelings by giving you assurance that somebody finds you sufficiently attractive to associate with you in an important setting.

53

Although the dating spectrum extends from a person's earliest dating experiences to the serious period of mate selection, the discussion here is limited to the uncommitted form of dating. This is called staccato or traveling dating, the opposite of going steady. The essence of it is to play the field far and wide, and to date as many partners as one can.

There are several advantages to dating a variety of partners. For one thing, it keeps you from getting tied down and becoming obligated to any one girl or boy. It is not only an exciting way of circulating and getting to know many new friends, but it also allows a person to broaden his own personality, thus eventually allowing him to explore and realize his own potential. It may also be true that having many dating partners is flattering to the ego, a way of sensing one's feelings of self-worth.

The Dating Dilemma

One thing which contributes to frustration on dates is not

knowing what to do. The following ideas may be of assistance to you.

DATING IN GRUBBIES

Go skydiving
Go for a bike ride up the canyons and have a picnic
Go horseback riding and play cops and robbers
Have a dog wash — wash the neighborhood dogs
Go rabbit hunting
Go sand jumping
Go ice skating or roller skating
Swing at the park
Visit your state capitol
Picket your own house
Go mountain climbing
Have a water-balloon fight
Go glacier sliding
Race toy trains
Build a dam in a stream or gutter
Ride a jeep to the top of a mountain and cook dinner
Paint a barn or a house
Fly toy or paper airplanes
Make mud pies and have a fight
Take a midnight hike with flashlights
Go bug collecting up the canyon
Take a sunrise hike and cook breakfast afterwards
Go graveyard walking
Go snipe hunting
Play in a fountain
Go on a scavenger hunt
Go skate board riding
Go river running
Play hopscotch in a parking lot
Have a house-cleaning party
Have a lawn-mowing and garage-cleaning party
Wash each other's cars
Rent hondas
Go on a hayride
Go to a wooded area and build a Robinson Crusoe hut
Play cowboys and Indians
Look for things at the city dump
Go caving and exploring
Go kite flying

54

Have a food or pie fight
Climb trees
Roll down hills
Go frog catching and have a frog jumping contest
Do a craft — make candles, macrame, fingerpaint
Ride the train at the zoo — have a picnic
Take bikes in a car to the top of mountain and ride down
Play croquet in the dark using flashlights
Get ice blocks and slide down grassy hills
Use a truck and set up a table in the back and have dinner
    (drive-in, parking lot, downtown)

CASUAL DATING

Visit Temple Square or the visitors center of your temple
Rent a truck or moving van and have a party in it
Have a candlelight dinner in mountains, at a parking terrace,
    etc.
Pick up date, go to show, window shop without use of car
Take sightseeing tour of city on a bus
Go elevator shopping
Visit a fish hatchery
Play "bird watching" at the aviary
Ride the Heber Creeper (or visit amusement park)
Cook dinner together
Go to a planetarium
Go to a symphony
Go to a melodrama
Fix popcorn and watch nightmare theater on TV
Visit the wax museum
Walk in the rain, fog, or snow
Visit travel agencies and plan a trip
Walk through Memory Grove and visit Charlie's bench
Go on the merry-go-round at a park
Go antique hunting
Go to the library, watch movie, or listen to records
Have a banana split-making contest
Shop for diamonds at jewelry stores
See what kind of good deed you can do for a quarter
Tour any historical sights in your area
Tour a mortuary
Visit a rest home with treats for the people
Buy ingredients and cook dinner for fifty cents a person

55

DRESSY

Go to breakfast in dinner clothes
Have a progressive dinner
Go to a hamburger drive-in in formals
Go to a play or symphony
Boys cook a formal dinner for girls, or vice versa
Have a chauffeur and red carpet treatment for dinner

MISCELLANEOUS

Ask a date by postcard or any unusual way: puzzle, cookie
    hunt, etc.
Play hide and seek in a department store
Play jacks or Risk at the airport
Have a birthday party for anyone, use strange utensils
Have a backwards party — menus, clothes, etc., all backwards
Go to a hotel lobby and watch television
Weave baskets
Kidnap your date
Teach boys to make bread or a cake
Bottle fruit in the summer
Go Christmas caroling in August
Have an Easter egg roll on public building steps
Roast hot dogs on the most appropriate fire you can find
Go to a drive-in, taking brothers and sisters along
Build an igloo
Color in coloring books
Watch the planes or trains come in
Go to the drag- or stock-car races
Play kick the can
Go people-watching and take notes
Sell bubblegum
Have an ice race with straws
Have a bubblegum-blowing contest
Go the fair
Go watch or participate in water skiing
Go wading in some unusual place
Get a team and play baseball, volleyball, etc., at night
Pop popcorn in the fireplace
Have a taffy pull
Go rowing or canoeing on the nearest lake
Tie a quilt

Make a home movie, write script, film, academy awards
Visit a ghost town
Make treats and leave them for people

Use your imagination, get permission (parents, owners, etc.),
use good taste and have a great time!

What Bugs You?

The dating experience, with its high priority in your social
life, contains trauma of many kinds. How to handle the
trauma may be difficult to determine by two young people
who are too involved in their relationship to "see the forest
for the trees." Because of this, I include the following list of
things you may be doing or that your partner may be doing
which "bug" the other. Many of these things are trivial, but
knowing one another's expectations about dating behavior
may allow you to have more rewarding and enjoyable dating
experiences.

57

Things that bother girls about what boys do on dates

Doesn't talk or carry on a conversation
Impolite, bad manners, won't open the door for you
Date isn't planned — boy doesn't make decision, but asks
    what you want to do
Aggressive, touchy
Talks about other girls
Insists on kissing
Shows off, sarcastic, big joker
Swears
Feels that he has to spend money or eat
Puts on an act
Thinks he is greater than you
Cuts himself down
Stands too long on the porch, won't leave
Drives too fast
Gives the other girls the eye on the date — flirts
Crude — burps, spits
Comes over with friends and whispers about you to them
Shy — won't touch you

Tries to impress you with car
Complains about how expensive the date is
Stays out too late
Calls your girl friend to ask if you like him
Can't stand silence
Always takes me to the same types of activities
Dates your good friend right after you stop going with him
Insists you sit next to him
Kisses you on the first date
Rude to you all during the date if you make one mistake
Doesn't ask you out after you have taken him out
Makes you order food first
Comes over to watch television — won't take you out
Insecure
Talks tough about drinking and smoking
Leaves you alone and talks to his friends
Too much after-shave
Doubles with people you don't know
Wears clothes which don't go together
Expects a performance from you as payment for his taking
    you out
Dirty fingernails
Doesn't shave
Too serious
Doubles with "lovey doveys"
Thinks you have a crush on him if you say "hi" to him
Always single dates
Talks too much
Embarrassed when his friends see him with you
After going together once, he follows you everywhere like he
    expects you to talk to him and be with him

Things that bother boys about what girls do on dates

Doesn't talk or carry on a conversation
Door hugger
Won't help make a decision on what to do — says, "I don't
    know"
Doesn't order dinner (she says no to eating, but is really
    hungry)
Talks about other boys
She's not ready for the date when you come to pick her up
Acts like she is doing you a favor by going out with you

Gossips about you
Expects you to be with her all the time
On double dates, the girls talk to the girls, and the boys have
    to talk to the boys
Gets up-tight over little things
Forward
Flirts with other guys on a date, or when she knows you're
    around
Says how fat or ugly she is
Acts dumb or bored
Wears gobs of make-up
Likes you for your money or your car
Always asks what time it is
Leads you on
Runs to the door after a date
Fixes her hair in the car
Refuses to talk about herself
Asks if you are mad at her
Always going to the restroom
Wears too much perfume
Complains about this and that
Giggles all of the time
Worries about how her clothes look
Puts on an act
Talks altogether too much
She thinks she is a "mover"
Smoking, drinking, swearing
Wears the wrong clothes for the date (formal clothes for
    casual dates, or vice versa)
Goofs off in a restaurant
Won't let you help her with her coat
Thinks you like her for security
No dresses; always pants, pants, pants
Won't tell you if she doesn't like you
Has her friends ask if you like her
Expects fancy dates
Goes on a date not expecting to have fun (duds)

Once when I was discussing the "dating game" with a
group of students in a dating and courtship setting, one of
them suggested that each person write down his biggest
hang-up about dating. Would you enjoy hearing what your

59

peers had to say? I have included their questions below in italics and followed them with my responses.

Why is there always such a big deal made about being sixteen years old before we can date?

It is ironic that this was also an area of great concern for my peer group. Those in the group who were allowed to date were always attempting to convince the rest of us that we were being dealt with unjustly.

Perhaps the soundest approach to take on the subject of what age you should begin dating would be to consider the counsel from our Church leaders. President Spencer W. Kimball, whom we sustain as a mouthpiece for our Father, has said: "When you get in the teen years, your social associations should still be a general acquaintance with both boys and girls. Any dating or pairing off in social contacts should be postponed until at least the age of sixteen or older, and even then there should be much judgment used in selections and in the seriousness." (Spencer W. Kimball, "The Marriage Decision," *Ensign* [Salt Lake City, February 1975], p. 4.)

Later in the year, in an address given to many of us who teach in the Seminary and Institute program, President Spencer W. Kimball restated his feelings about early dating when he said: "It's sad to find children marrying and having families while they're still children. . . . Any dating or pairing off in social context should be deferred until the high school years. Even then, great care should be taken to use judgment in the selection of those whose company we keep." (Spencer W. Kimball, Seminar for Seminary and Institute Personnel, Salt Lake City, September 1975.)

It is interesting that our prophet mentions the age of sixteen in one address and uses the term "high school years" in the other. Many will grasp onto the latter statement as license for early dating. I believe that if you want to pair off in a dating relationship early in your teen years, you will go ahead and do it regardless of the counsel you receive. On the other hand, I salute those of you who are grateful for the direction and concern of our prophet. It is admirable that even though you may not understand all of the reasons for certain counsel, you are desirous of being obedient and receptive in your lives.

It is my observation that there are two types of attitudes among the young people in the Church today. There are those who say, "I believe the things that I am being taught, *however* . . ." There are others who say, "I believe the things that I am being taught, *therefore* . . ."

Do you see the difference? If you are a person who constantly struggles with parental guidance or with advice from Church leaders, perhaps it is time to step back and take a good long look at what you are becoming. You are right now molding and shaping yourself into the type of adult that you will become.

61

The concern your parents and leaders have about early dating stems from their observation of the consequences of dating early. Those who begin dating early are those who want to go steady early, and those who date just one on a steady basis become bored with little or no physical attention. They then allow themselves to increase their physical involvement with their steady date until they find themselves ensnared in an ugly and immoral relationship.

Perhaps President Kimball summed it up when he said, "It's sad to find children marrying and having families while they're still children."

This is not to say that sixteen is the magic age for all young people to start to date. Your parents should be close enough to each of you to provide personal direction. They understand better than anyone else your maturity, judgment, and personal capabilities. Many are not ready to date even at age sixteen.

Always be grateful for the direction you receive, seek counsel and direction from your parents and those who know you best, and, most importantly, become one of those much-appreciated individuals who say, "I believe the things I am being taught, *therefore* . . ."

How can you let a guy know you like him without chasing him away?

One of the excitements of dating is likewise one of the hazards. Dating is truly a "game," at least during the early stages. Girls have been struggling with this dilemma for thousands of years!

One of the patterns of early dating is the cat and mouse game. A boy will like a certain girl until he finds that she likes him, or vice versa. The most reassuring thing I can say is that when you grow older and begin dating for the purpose of mate selection, you will find that your relationships last longer, become more meaningful, and consequently become less of a game. In a mature relationship, both partners sense an excitement as well as a security in knowing the feelings each has for the other.

What do boys look for in girls?

This question is posed more often than any other by girls as they reach for identity and for acceptance. My response may seem antiquated as well as trite, but from discussions with young men, the following traits surface in order of their importance to young men: First, be a "real" person. It's true — no one likes a "phony" or a "put on." Incidentally, those who are unreal usually find their first date their last as well.

Girls who are feminine are much appreciated. It was quite an eye-opener for me to begin teaching in Salt Lake

62

City and notice that almost all of the girls in seminary wore casual pants or levis most of the time. This was so intriguing to me that I thought it worth some class discussion. I discovered that most girls wore jeans regularly simply because everyone else wore them. Out of 127 girls, 11 had never worn a dress to school, 19 had attended school in a dress fewer than ten times a year, and 115 wore pants more often than they did a dress.

The most surprising thing they learned was that most of the young men polled would have preferred that the girls wear dresses most of the time.

A lot of emphasis is put on clothes, but there is more to it than that. Young men are attracted to those who are feminine in their manner as well as their apparel. Have you found that you act the way you look? If this is so, you will act like young ladies when you look the part. I have noticed that other than wearing apparel, the way a girl cares for her hair is the most important determiner of behavior. When a girl ceases to care for her hair, her personal hygiene also suffers, and her chances for social acceptance become slim. Be proud to be a young lady!

63

Should you kiss on the first date?

Are you ready for this? The answer is simple and unwavering — *no!* A thousand times *no!*

If we were to look at what the world does, we would find that a kiss on the first date is very acceptable. Just looking at the mass media — magazines, movies, television — as well as "in person" examples around us, we find perfectly imperfect examples of how to treat a kiss. Studies point out that young people who think casual kissing is an acceptable social gesture soon become bored with a simple kiss. When it loses its true value, increased physical involvement occurs.

Young men, if you desire to impose yourself upon a young lady regardless of her wishes, just to receive a physical thrill or to prove how manly you are or whatever your intention, you are assuming too much. If you truly respect and honor a young lady, you will want to do everything in your power to keep her free from tarnish. Some have thought me very old-fashioned, but it is my philosophy that if you are a true gentleman, you will ask a young lady before you kiss her. By doing this, you are clearly saying to her that you respect her as a person, with rights and standards, and that you do not consider her a mere object for your desires.

Young ladies, ofttimes young men are given the full responsibility or blame for when a kiss is given. This should not be so. Even though you may not want to kiss a fellow, you sometimes lead him on throughout the evening (for social acceptance or other reasons), then you think he is out of line to want to kiss you at the end of the date.

Just when does a kiss become appropriate?

There is no pat answer for this question. It must be considered on an individual basis. Not long ago I attended a banquet where a college football coach was speaking. He mentioned that one of his players, who was named All-American, was highly respected by his teammates. He said that as this young man began dating his future companion, together they agreed not to kiss until their marriage at the altar in the temple. Feeling that a kiss was this special and sacred, they set this as their goal and reached that goal.

Certainly this is unusual, yet the important point is that they shared the same values, and together allowed the kiss to become a very special event in their relationship. Because of this, it will always be a very special symbol of their love for each other.

I believe that a kiss should be reserved for someone who means a great deal to you. If you allow it to become sacred and special, it will provide that much more meaning as you begin your eternal marriage with the one you love.

One young lady came into my office with the concern that the only type of boy she could attract was the "mover." I asked her how free she was with her affections. She knew what I was driving at. Although it hurt her to admit it, her pattern was to make out with anyone she dated.

As you know, each of you has a reputation which you either live up to or live down to. Your actions on dates will soon establish your reputation with your peers.

It was Ninon De L'Enclos who said, "That which is striking and beautiful is not always good; but that which is good is always beautiful." If you hold sacred the kiss, as well as other affections, you will be good in our Father's eyes, and beautiful to yourself and to those who mean the most to you.

65

What do you think about dating someone who is not of our faith?

This has to be one of the most perplexing problems that parents must deal with. It is also a question which almost all teenagers must resolve.

It is true that you will marry those with whom you associate. *It is true* that you will become like the person you marry. *It is true* that you cannot expect to change your spouse after marriage. Therefore, marry him (or her) with this expectation. *It is also true* that "a candle loses nothing by lighting another candle."

What, then, are you to do?

It has been my observation that young people who marry out of their own faith immediately have a strike against the solidarity of their relationship. More often than not this becomes a thorn in their marriage, particularly when children come along. Ofttimes this problem becomes so acute as to be one of the wounds which causes the marriage to die. This is particularly so when one or both partners feel strongly about their own religion.

I have also seen many outstanding young people accept the gospel after being introduced to it by someone they knew and cared for on a dating basis. Because of these observations, I have adopted the following philosophy which I often share with young people who are in this dilemma.

If you are just beginning to date, or if you are dating simply for fun and enjoyment as well as personal development, casually dating someone of another faith can become a "light their candle" experience. If, however, you are in your late teen years or older, use a great deal of discretion. Perhaps the most important thing for you to remember is that your parents love you more than anyone does. They also know you more thoroughly, *and* they have been given a stewardship over you. Such love, knowledge and stewardship gives parents special insight and understanding into your personality, your needs, and your capabilities. You will do well to seek their counsel if this question applies to you.

How do you politely say no to a boy who has asked you out a number of times but you don't want to accept a date?"

The answer to this problem is contained in chapter 3, where emotional honesty and emotional maturity were discussed.

Being emotionally honest is making the decision to always "say it like it is." Emotionally mature means you are mature enough to handle an honest expression of emotions that you may give or receive.

Regardless of how socially mature a young lady is, there is the temptation of telling a "white" lie (if there is such a thing) when she doesn't want to date a boy. The sad thing is that if a girl constantly makes up shallow excuses, a boy usually persists in asking for dates, causing the experience to repeat itself again and again.

If you are dating one fellow, but someone else is persistent in asking you out, simply tell the persistent one that you are flattered he would ask you out, but that you like someone else. If you can do so honestly, tell him you would rather be on a friend basis than a dating basis with him.

Believe it or not, boys appreciate a girl who is honest enough to tell him the truth rather than making up excuse after excuse for not going with him. Boys do not like to be led on any more than do girls. Say it like it is — in a tactful and polite manner — and you will be glad you did.

67

Because my parents don't like my boy friend, they make it really difficult for me. They don't know him very well, but because I'm getting serious with him, they say that I am too young, and won't even try to get to know him or accept him.

Perhaps the parents in question aren't really against the boy friend, but simply object to their daughter's steady dating at this point in her life.

Here's a suggestion for each of you. When you feel a communication gap developing between you and your parents, take the initiative to go to them with your feelings. Allow parents the courtesy of expressing their feelings, and no doubt they will offer the same courtesy to you. When parents find that you are capable of discussing a problem in a mature manner, they begin to have more trust and confidence in you, and begin treating you on an adult basis.

It is a real hassle when my parents go through the "board of review" questions:

>*Is he a Mormon?*
>*What is he like?*
>*Are his parents active in the Church?*
>*What kind of boys does he hang around?*
>*Does he go to seminary?*
>*How long is his hair?*

Every time it's the same darn thing! I wonder if they are ever going to trust me in this kind of decision!

Although it may be difficult for you to believe, there are two different reasons parents assume this posture regarding your dating relationships. One or both reasons may exist in your particular case.

68

It may help you understand if you try and place yourself in your parents' shoes. The first reason is positive, and should make you feel grateful for parents who sincerely feel this way.

(1) Most parents are genuinely concerned. Regardless of who you are going out with — they want the best for you. The answers to their questions provide a signal to them (in their list of priorities) as to the type of person you are dating.

(2) The second reason they ask these questions could be because of your previous dating record. If you have given your parents cause for concern by dating questionable people, they will "hassle" you. I have found that those of you who gain the trust and respect of your parents do not receive constant questioning from them.

My biggest problem is trying to explain to the person I have dated for quite a while that I want to begin dating others as well.

Especially in early dating relationships is this a problem. It is often most difficult for a young lady to be in this position, as she cannot simply snap her fingers and have another date. A steady relationship offers a girl security that is easy to become quite dependent upon.

If you are a young man, simply tell your partner your feelings. If she is sensitive to your wishes (and if she still wants to date you), she will give you this freedom. The worst thing a dating partner can do is to try to hang on when the other person wants some freedom. Feelings cannot be forced!

Establish Ideals

As you reflect upon the issues just discussed, please consider them without becoming defensive. A great deal has been said about heeding the counsel and advice of parents. Perhaps you can best understand parents' feelings as you read this poem.

69

I must not interfere with my child, I have been told,
To bend his will to mine, or try to shape him through some
    mold of thought.
Naturally, as a flower, he must unfold.
Yet, flowers have the discipline of wind and rain;
And, though I know it gives the gardener pain,
I've seen him use his pruning shears to gain
Strength and beauty for blossoms rare.
Thus he tends what's in his care
As the Master-florist tends his lilies fair.
I do not know, yet it seems to me,
That only weeds are left to unfold naturally.

— Author unidentified

One young friend came to see me not long ago, crying a bucket of tears. She was in the process of breaking up with her steady boy friend because she had finally come to realize that he was like an unpruned weed. Not only was he destroy-

ing himself, but his influence was beginning to kill her desire to remain true to the principles she had been taught. Although a member of the Church, he no longer honored his priesthood. Rather, he scoffed at her for the priorities she had established in her life. You see, he had been left by his parents to unfold naturally, with virtually no restraints.

It is frightening to see how easily we are influenced by the fads of the day. Every change in fashion makes us want to change our wardrobe or our hairstyle or perhaps even our thinking. A new dance comes along and we have to adopt it in order to be accepted.

No doubt change is an important element of progress, and justifiable in many aspects of the dating experience. It is essential, however, to guard against many of the superficialities of life that could change your goals, your ideals, your standards.

71

An interesting illustration of this point is found in the ocean when the ice is breaking up. You can observe the wind, the waves, and the surface ice moving in one direction, yet in the center of the movement you can see an iceberg moving serenely in the opposite direction. The explanation for this phenomenon is that the deeper currents are not influenced by the wind and surface ice. Since the iceberg extends deep into the ocean, it is able to move quietly on its chosen course.

So it is with you. If you are well-rooted in your principles, you will not be influenced by every wind that blows, but will continue on your chosen course.

Chapter 7

This Thing Called Love

Lowell Bennion said, "Love is not looking at each other, but looking out and up together."

There are many different types of love, including love for God, love for parents and children, love for brothers and sisters, love for self, and charity, which is "the pure love of Christ." This chapter will concentrate on love as it develops on a romantic basis.

As you develop the ability to love, you will become aware of the importance of being mentally active, receptive, and sensitive in your interactions with others. As Latter-day Saints, you have a particular advantage in coming to understand the different facets of love. You have parents and Church leaders who are concerned, and who place the guidelines constantly before you.

Just what is romantic love? Perhaps you visualize it as being the feelings which exist between husband and wife and as the ideal in love for the opposite sex. In some relationships romantic love is all that exists. I happen to picture romantic love as being the prelude to real love.

When two people begin dating, they may first experience the "fluttering heart" feeling, which may quickly blossom

into romantic love. If the relationship is allowed to deepen and become more meaningful, the romantic feelings begin to expand and take on additional meaning. When real love develops, a couple does not have to be wrapped up in each other's arms to experience the joys of their relationship. They become excited and involved with helping the partner realize his or her potential. This feeling takes on added meaning for a couple as they share the birth of each of their children.

A good friend of mine once expressed his feeling that love is not a discovery, but is truly an art. We do not merely "fall" into real love, but only through sharing and giving can we develop the art of loving.

Based on my studies and observation, I believe there are basically two different philosophies of love. Many people believe that we love those who satisfy our needs, while others feel that we satisfy the needs of those we love. While there are many whose love for their spouse would fall in either of these categories, the second one reflects a more mature and gospel-oriented type of love than does the first.

As you try to develop meaningful relationships, keep in mind these ideas. Be careful not to become so self-oriented that you are only concerned with having your own needs fulfilled. You will find that as you concern yourself with fulfilling the needs of your dating partners, this will eventually become a very natural part of your personality. When this happens, you will search for a mate with the same orientation.

False Loves

As you begin to flex your social muscles, you will find yourself caught up in the elation of being in love. Here is a verse that portrays this euphoric feeling.

73

I ran up the door
And closed the stairs,
Said my pajamas
And put on my prayers.
Turned off my bed
And jumped into the light,
And all because
You kissed me good-night!

— *Author unidentified*

Even though you may not be truly in love, there is value in having these experiences. You become excited about forming relationships, and this is essential if you expect to have a happy and fulfilling marriage. By way of complementing the above poem, someone once offered this as a definition of love: "Love is a feeling that you feel when you feel that you're going to feel a feeling that you've never felt before!"

There are primarily three types of false loves. These include falling in love with love, falling in love with being loved, and infatuation.

You may know someone who is constantly falling in love with love. Such a person is either so desperate for affection, or so shallow in his ability to form meaningful relationships that he simply falls in love with anyone. There are many young people who "must" have a boy friend or a girl friend. They actually do not love the person, but love "love" itself.

The second type of false love, falling in love with being loved, is a need-fulfilling experience. This is apparent with those who are unable to develop significant relationships. More often than not, such a person is lacking love in his home or in peer relationships, and so is grasping for any type of relationship, even though it might be temporary or one-sided. There is social security in this type of love.

The last type of false love is often mentioned when considering immature and shallow relationships. This, of course, is infatuation. To help you more fully understand the

differences between infatuation and love, check these comparisons:

INFATUATION	LOVE
Tends to be more frequent among young adolescents in early teens	Tends to occur first in late teens and in the twenties
Frequently being involved with more than one boy or girl friend	Not frequently going with more than one partner
Tends to last but a short time (usually only a few weeks)	Most cases last over a long period of time
Often happens soon after a previous involvement has ended	More slowly develops after a love affair has ended
Is often the name given to past relationships	Often used to refer to present affair
Focuses more frequently on an unsuitable person	Usually refers to a suitable person
Parents often call it this when they disapprove	Parents tend to approve
Focuses on a few traits; mostly physical thrill	Broadly involves the entire personality
Less frequently accompanied by ambition and wide interests	Brings new energy and ambition and more interest in life
Feelings of guilt, insecurity and frustration are frequent	Associated with feelings of self-confidence, trust and security
Tends to be self-centered and restricted	Accompanied by kindlier feelings toward others in general

75

INFATUATION	LOVE
Boredom is frequent when there is no sexual excitement or social amusement	Joy in many common interests and an ongoing sense of being alive when going together — precludes boredom
Little change in relationship with the passing of time	Relationship changes and grows with further association, developing interest, and deepening feelings
Problems and barriers are often disregarded; problems are idealized rather than faced with reality	Accompanied by willingness to face reality and to tackle problems realistically
Almost always leaps quickly into bloom	Usually takes root slowly and it always grows with time
Usually accompanied with a sense of uncertainty; you are stimulated and thrilled, but you are not really happy; you are filled with feverish excitement; you are miserable when he is absent	You have a calmness about your relationship. You have a deeper excitement that dwells on the meaningful relationship you have, rather than always being in the other's presence
You often lose your appetite. You just don't want food. You can't study. You can't keep your mind on your work. You're mostly likely short-tempered and rather unpleasant with the family	You have your "emotional" head on your shoulders. You work harder because of life's meaning. You are happy and pleasant to be around
Brings the feeling that you must get married right away. You can't wait — you must not take the chance of losing him or her	Though you may prefer to marry at once, you know that you can wait. You are sure of one another. You plan your future with complete confidence

76

INFATUATION	LOVE
Actually stems from a desire for self-gratification. The young man or woman is often a "hero" and popular person in your crowd. Or this person may be brilliant and you wish identity with him. You want others to know that you have been chosen by this person	There is always deep concern for the welfare of the loved one. Outside criticism does not dull your attachment. It sharpens it. Misfortune which may take away his or her "hero" status is of no consequence to you
Largely a matter of sex. If you are honest, you will discover that it may be difficult to enjoy each other unless you are leading up to necking	Sex is a natural and spontaneous part of love, but only a part. If your love is real, you will enjoy comradeship with the loved one. You can have fun together without necking. You are friends as well as lovers. You like each other
Infatuated couples find it easy to disagree	When in love, although your personalities may be quite different, there is a willingness to hear the other side; to give as well as to take; to compromise
Frequently brings with it the inability to trust the partner. When away from you, you wonder if your partner is with another girl or boy friend. You're jealous when your partner laughs with another person or dances with them. You wonder how much you can believe of what your partner has told you	Love understands that your partner may enjoy another dance, another laugh, with no reflection upon the relationship with you. There is a sense that you each belong to each other, that all others are outside
You may "fall" into infatuation	You never "fall" in love, but rather you grow in love

77

INFATUATION	LOVE
Might possibly lead you to do things of which you would not ordinarily approve — things for which you would be sorry later	Love will cause you to respect and trust your partner, and therefore will not allow you to dishonor your partner or yourself. Love leads you up. It makes you look up. It makes you think up. It makes you a better person than you were before

In the comparisons above we touched upon the matter of sex as it relates to infatuation and love. In the additional comparative list below, take a closer look at relationships which are sex-oriented compared with those which are centered around love:

SEX	LOVE
A biological need	A psychological need
Experienced primarily in the erotic zones of the body	Involvement of the total personality
Objectless — anyone will do	Searches for a specific personality
Found in both man and beast	Found only in humans — but not all humans
Very impersonal and casual	Very personal
The partner can become of no account, boring or even hateful after satisfaction is reached	The partner is important whether or not there is satisfaction
One looks for different physical characteristics in a sex partner	One looks for both mental and physical characteristics in a love partner

SEX	LOVE
Selfish, seeks personal satisfaction	Concerned with welfare and happiness of partner. Fears calamity or danger for partner
Partner is idolized — something to worship	Partner is idealized — someone to be admired, to become like
Doesn't share pain or joy when other person experiences them	Shares all emotion experienced by the other person
Possible to possess the other person, to force affections upon them	Impossible to possess other person or to force other person to love you
Concerned only with parts of the body	Concerned with heart, mind — the total person
Variety of partners possible — they are easily replaced	Variety much less possible — Partner is difficult to replace
Desire comes and goes — Very dependent upon moods	Desire remains constant, not dependent upon moods
Deteriorates with age	Grows with age

79

There are two reasons for sharing this comparison with you. First, some of you may now be or may in the future be involved in a sex-oriented relationship. I hope that by recalling the things you have just read you will have the fortitude to climb out of that losing relationship, no matter how imposing your partner is.

The second reason is that you may be caught in the trap of seeking only physical thrills in the relationships you form. You may think that you are well on your way in preparing for marriage. Think about what you have just read. These things have not been fabricated to give you a "snow job."

The things you have read do hold water; they are *true!* I can promise you that if you stubbornly cling to relationships which are sex-oriented, which contain the attributes of infatuation, such relationships will be temporary and only partially fulfilling at best. On the other hand, if you develop the attributes of love in the relationships you form, you will stand a much greater chance of having a happy and satisfying and lasting marriage with the one you truly love.

The Unloving

I would like to flip the coin now and expose you to the characteristics of those people who find it difficult to love. As you become acquainted with these ideas, think of those around you who have difficulty developing lasting relationships, and see if these characteristics fit them. As you do so, consider the comments below, made on the basis of a discussion of this subject in K. L. Cannon's book.

These unloving individuals have few or no friends. They find what is wrong with people more quickly than they find what is right with them. They tend to hold themselves aloof, to withdraw. Such a person may make an exception of you and pour all of his love out in your direction if you have a great capacity for love.

Another sign of inability to love is to feel that "nobody loves me," "nobody understands me." The person who feels misunderstood is the one who very often doesn't understand or try to understand others. When we say that nobody loves us or that nobody understands us, chances are that we are the ones who do not understand others.

Excessive ambition is a further indication of being unable to love. Closely related to this characteristic is the need for an unloving person to be a perfectionist. Since he knows the right way and he cannot tolerate the wrong way, he will love only if his beloved is perfect. He cannot tolerate the foibles of people; in short, he cannot tolerate his partner.

An unloving person is often one who is unable to say no. This person very frequently appears to be loving, but he feels a compulsion to please everybody, mostly out of fear of rejection should he refuse.

A final characteristic of the unloving is that of self-absorption. It is true that a person must have a good self-image, and hold himself in high esteem. Self-absorption is just the opposite. A person is so absorbed in his own problems that he has little concern for others, for what he can contribute to others, or for what he can feel with others. When an individual accepts himself, his attention and efforts are released to focus upon others. When he can extend his vision to care for others, he can then be a loving person. (Cannon, *Developing a Marriage Relationship,* p. 2.)

As you have considered these characteristics, you may have said to yourself: "That's me. It fits me to a *T*." Don't be too harsh on yourself. Everyone has moments like this — even the most confident, secure, popular, friendly, loving person. So hang in there and get involved with people and their feelings. It is exciting to learn to love others as you listen, feel, and empathize with them. I challenge you to learn to do things for others, for it is through giving and serving that love comes back to you.

81

"Am I Really in Love?"

This question is surely asked at one time or another before the mirror of almost every home in the world. Here are some guidelines that should be helpful to you as you consider this eternity-based question.

Real love includes a strong feeling toward a person based on sharing fundamental goals, aims, and standards in life. You will find that attraction grows as you and your partner discover common ground in your life's values.

Real love surfaces when you feel that a person would make an excellent father or mother of your children. Though many of you have never thought of this, it is very important. Some people who are ardent lovers and "Don Juan" sweethearts are complete failures as parents. One test of true love is whether or not you would sincerely want this person to become the father or mother of your children.

A couple in love develops a "we" feeling. As they come closer together they do more planning and thinking about the two as a unit and less about themselves as individuals. If you are marrying mainly because you want to be happy and are little concerned about the welfare of your sweetheart, you do not have the kind of love that produces a harmonious marriage. Genuine love is unselfish and shared. The welfare of the team is all-important.

When you are in love, you think as much of the other person as you do of yourself. You should have high esteem for yourself, but in a successful marriage you will need to feel just as strongly toward your mate; otherwise, when conflicts and differences arise, serious problems will begin to surface.

When you truly love someone, you would rather be with that person than with anyone you know, including parents, relatives or friends. Husband-wife relationships are among the most precious known to man. The scriptures support this idea with the advice that a man should leave his mother and father and "cleave unto his wife: and they shall be one flesh." (Genesis 2:24.)

When love is real, your partner is a genuine companion to you. This means on an apron-and-overall basis, not just when it's party time. Real sweethearts feel comfortable together and enjoy each other's company in simple, everyday activities.

To love someone, a romantic attraction must be present. This is not enough by itself, but when it accompanies other favorable characteristics it adds warmth and zest to a marriage.

Couples in love should meet on common ground mentally, socially, and spiritually. While this does not mean that two persons must have identical interests and activities, it has been found that the more a couple has in common, the better their chances are for a happy and satisfying marriage.

It is my expectation that you have now gained greater insight into love and its many facets. David O. McKay once said, "The ability to love and to give is the highest ideal ever given to man." It is my hope that you will cultivate these truths, and that they will assist you as you search out and find the mate who will become your companion for eternity. As you do, reflect upon these words:

"Love is a great thing, a good above all others, which alone maketh every burden light . . . Love is watchful, and while sleeping, still keeps watch; though fatigued, it is not weary; though pressed, it is not forced. Love is sincere, gentle, strong, patient, faithful, prudent, long-suffering, and manly. Love is humble and upright; not weak, not fickle, nor intent on vain things; sober, chaste, steadfast, quiet, and guarded in all the senses." (Thomas a Kempis.)

83

You have gained much if you now realize that love is learned. We all pass through stages of learning as we reach for "true" love. Perhaps you have been infatuated, or have been in love with love, or have loved being loved. You may have even felt unloving at times, and wondered if you could ever *really* love someone enough to fulfill their needs. These feelings are very natural. Almost all of us experience them. The development of real love could be compared to climbing a ladder and reaching a higher form of love at the top. It is my hope that you will marry when you are high on that ladder and that you will continue climbing and growing together until you reach celestial heights.

Chapter 8

Surviving Satan's Subtleties

President David O. McKay said: "The flower by the roadside that catches the dust of every traveler is not the one to be admired and is seldom, if ever, plucked; but one blooming away up on the hillside, protected by a perpendicular cliff, is the flower with the virgin perfume, the one the boy will almost risk his life to possess." (David O. McKay, *Gospel Ideals* [Salt Lake City: Improvement Era, 1953], p. 451.)

It would be inviting to think that we could all grow into adulthood without the subtle temptations placed in our path by Satan. Just imagine walking into the temple as perfect as the day we were born, ready to take upon ourselves the responsibility of a new family unit. But would we really be ready if we had not experienced difficulties and opposition? Consider this poem:

> It's easy enough to be virtuous,
> When nothing tempts you to stray,
> When without and within no voice of sin
> Is luring your soul away;
> But it's only a negative virtue
> Until it is tried by fire.
> And the soul that is worth the blessings of earth
> Is the soul that resists desire.
>
> — *Ella Wheeler Wilcox*

Where, then do you draw the line? Do you allow yourself to get into awkward and improper situations so that you can master your weaknesses? As we both know, it isn't that easy. You are constantly bombarded by temptations, regardless of your efforts to maintain a distance from them.

As you consider your worth as an individual, as well as your potential, consider also your most precious possession. President Hugh B. Brown stated: "The richest diadem in the world is worn only by the pure in heart. It is a priceless jewel, a gift from heaven bestowed on all at birth. In life's crucible it is smelted, burnished, made to sparkle, and its worth is enhanced by time. Though it is fragile, it should not be kept in a glass showcase like the crown jewels. Its value is increased by wearing. There is a distinction between innocence and purity. One is passive and the other active." (Hugh B. Brown, *You and Your Marriage* [Salt Lake City: Bookcraft, Inc., 1960], p. 67.) To be innocent requires no effort; to remain pure amidst the temptations of the world requires a constant vigil.

Several years ago, as I prepared for combat in Viet Nam, I was taught a principle of survival that is worth repeating. We learned that the most successful method of our enemies was to capitalize on the element of surprise. They would attack when and where they were least expected. As a result, thousands of injuries and deaths were incurred needlessly.

In order to defend ourselves from the element of surprise, we were repeatedly drilled on maintaining the "on guard" position while in a combat situation. We learned that it was essential for survival. In developing combat readiness, we also learned various techniques that we could implement according to the situation. We first learned hand-to-hand combat, but we also learned that it was to be used as a last resort. The second technique we learned was fighting with the bayonet. The various strokes with that weapon were effective only when we were taking the offensive in the "on guard" position.

85

During our training we constantly felt the stress placed on us by our instructors. They emphasized that on the battlefield our attitude could lead to our death or our survival. At the time it meant very little to many of us. You see, we were on a training ground twelve thousand miles away from a war that we might never see.

Not until orders came through sending all but ten of us to Southeast Asia did we sober to what was ahead. It is not a secret that many of my buddies died in Viet Nam — some of them needlessly — because they were not prepared.

Are You Ready for Battle?

So it is with you. Right now you are taking your basic training. You are being taught the finer points of combat, the use of all the weapons there are in the war against Satan. As a last resort you are even taught hand-to-hand combat! The most crucial instruction you receive, however, is the necessity for becoming combat-ready by maintaining an "on guard" position, never letting down your defenses, for if you do, it will surely lead to your spiritual death.

Because you are on the battlefield even today, the purpose of this chapter is threefold: First, to provide adequate and essential ammunition to help you to survive; second, to motivate you to maintain a constant vigil over your spiritual lives; and third, to assist any of you who may lie, even now, wounded by the subtleties of the destroyer.

It was just a decade ago that I walked in your shoes, but so many changes have taken place in our environment since then that it is hardly recognizable. Unfortunately, many of those changes are not for the best. Never before has a generation been forced to cope with so many social impositions. Never before has Satan held such an edge in his war against truth, and his war against youth.

Your Image

If you really want to one day join a companion, and together successfully rear children as our Father would have you do, the word *maturity* will not turn you off. You simply cannot chance your way through these critical years and hope the chips will fall for the best.

One of the easiest ways for you to measure your personal maturity is to measure your attitude. What is important to you? How do your parents come across to you? How do your closest friends react to you? What are you noted for around school? What is your reputation? How do you feel about *you?* All of these things reflect your attitude.

Not long ago a student came to see me who seemed very concerned that he didn't have any close friends. Actually, he had one friend — a person with whom he didn't enjoy associating. I asked him why he palled around with that fellow if it wasn't rewarding for him to do so. His response was that no one else seemed interested in him, so he had no other choice. I knew his friend, as I had seen them together at school and at ball games, so I asked him what there was about his friend that turned him off.

87

He said that he was repulsed by the way this fellow looked and smelled. His friend rarely bathed, almost never shaved, seldom combed his hair, and he wore a "dinner" jacket — one with food spilled down the front, a new layer each day.

The ironic thing was this: this student was not only describing his friend, he was unknowingly describing himself. I suggested this to him, and thank goodness he was my friend. He made a resolve then and there to straighten up his act.

Now to talk about you young ladies. I'd like to share an experience with you that happened not long ago when I began teaching in the seminary program. My first assignment was in Phoenix, Arizona. As school began, I was taken back by the overly casual manner in which the girls dressed. I soon learned that there was a great deal of peer pressure to dress immodestly. A true barometer of student feelings soon surfaced in the form of an editorial in the school paper.

HOT TEMPERATURES HEAT CODE ISSUE

"With temperatures rising, the dress code controversy of what to wear and bare has hit the campus.

"Students complain, 'It isn't fair.' Asked if we should have a dress code, one said, 'I think it stinks, especially in this weather. . . .'

"One girl who dared to wear the forbidden attire fumed. 'I wore a halter top to school and it did not disrupt one of my classes, nor did it offend one person, so I would say that it kind of defeats the dress code's purposes, wouldn't you say?'

"An unidentified student replied, 'They have a right to show off and wear anything. It's their body!'

"Perhaps [name] summed it all up by saying, 'Nope. I don't like the rules at all, because this is a free country. . . .'

"Regardless of what the students think, the administration is not altering any facet to the dress code for next year, but if the lack of enforcement by the administration continues and students keep violating dress code rules, administration may change their mind. . . ." (M. Hansen, "Hot Temperatures Heat Code Issue," *Panther Tracks,* Vol. 11, 1973. Phoenix, Arizona, Newspaper, p. 1.)

After we read this article in class, a heated discussion ensued. It became apparent that even some of these special young Latter-day Saints were so influenced by their peers that the teachings they had received at home and church were (in the heat of the battle) being tossed aside.

Thank goodness those young people were pliable enough in their thinking that when they heard the truth they responded. To illustrate their response, here is a letter that one young lady wrote to me not long after that discussion. She has granted me permission to share this with you:

"Even now when I choose a pattern for a dress or something, I remember those things you told me about a man's thoughts, and how if I am purposely causing those thoughts the sin is partially on my head. That's a scary thing. Look how long I've been wearing those kinds of clothes and how many men I come in contact with each day. Boy! Have I got a lot of repenting to do!

"I am seriously thinking about getting my patriarchal blessing. I don't want to get it too early, but I don't want to wait too much longer, either.

"Well, guess what? I finally went on my first date! It was really neat. Not because the guy was someone that I've got a mad crush on, because he's not. It's because I thought enough of myself to be choosy about the type of guy I go out with. This guy I went out with is so much more spiritual, morally clean, and decent than any other guy that has asked me out. I'm so thankful that I did not go out with just anybody that asked, because I've kept my reputation clean, gotten my parent's respect and trust, and I can feel good about myself.

"I once heard a man named Don Black say this about dating: 'If, after you come home from a date, you think about the person you've been out with from the neck up, you know you've had a good experience. But if all you can see is from the neck down, something has gone wrong.' It's a very good way to tell how you are doing in your dating experiences.

"Another good thing to do is pray, just before your date comes. This way you can ask for the Spirit of the Lord and his protection."

It is exciting to realize that your Heavenly Father has the same feelings of pride and esteem for you when you respond to his Spirit as do your earthly parents. Dare to take a stand and remain different — and exciting — and beautiful —and worthy!

Dating Behavior

If you want to see if you are in this "on guard" position, step back and look at yourself in a social setting with a partner.

89

After leaving Phoenix, I was assigned to teach at East High Seminary in Salt Lake City, Utah. One of the district seminary functions in this area was to sponsor a yearly seminary "S" Day and computer dance. This proved to be a very interesting phenomenon for my wife and me.

The day approached, and excitement was almost electric as my students received computer cards giving their date's phone number. The boys all rushed to the various school yearbooks in hopes of spotting the girl of their dreams. For the girls, anxiety ran rampant. "Will he call me?" "What if he sees my picture?" "Which school will he be from?" "What will we talk about for a whole three hours?" "Will we go out to dinner at McDonalds, or what?" "Will my dress turn out like I want it?" "Will we dance, or will we just walk laps around the mall where the dance is being held?" "Oh, I wish I'd never signed up!" "What if he holds my hand?"

Saturday came. The sun reflected warmly on the kitchen window that late winter morning in February. Gulping down my morning eggnog, I couldn't help feeling excited that this was my first "S" Day in the Salt Lake Valley. As we climbed into the car, I mentioned to my wife how neat it was that we were beginning this day with a devotional in the Tabernacle with Elder Paul H. Dunn. A great way to begin a day as promising as this one!

The devotional was even greater than our expectations. The "dessert" for that hour was listening intently and with pride as the combined seminary choirs sang "I Am a Child of God."

The day progressed without mishap as we saw the movie "Jeremiah Johnson," and then prepared for the dance. I remember purchasing six rolls of thirty-six-exposure film. I just had to capture some of the expressions on my students' faces as they came into the dance. Nor was I disappointed. We saw some very uncomfortable young men and women nervously entering the mall, some with looks of despair; others with looks of fright; all making the attempt to be "cool" with a date of such status.

What a hoot! My primary concern as I snapped their pictures was that they would become well enough acquainted to have a halfway memorable evening. And then the bomb dropped!

Tucking away the last roll of exposed film, we stashed the camera and headed for the dance floor. A slow dance was just beginning, which suited us fine. We weren't up to the fast dancing the students did. I took my dear wife's hand and onto the floor we went. What a special feeling to be dancing with the one I loved, the one who was mine for eternity. I'm sure that all of my students were in pure agony, having to dance a slow dance. For a few seconds we danced, eyes closed, enjoying the moment.

It suddenly dawned on me that we might not be setting the proper example, and so one eye opened, then two eyes. Then I blinked — and blinked again. I couldn't believe what I was seeing!

91

We were in the middle of the dance floor, surrounded by young people who had known each other for an hour and a half at the most, and each of these couples were melted together into a single form. Even more startling was the fact that there was virtually no movement on the dance floor. We might have been standing on a thousand doorsteps watching couples embrace as though they were getting married the following Saturday!

And then I panicked! What to do? Should we resume dancing in our old-fashioned, conventional way, do we continue to stare, or do we work our way through this entranced group of "no more strangers"? Social pressure gave way to sentiment as we decided we needed a drink! We were so shocked that we didn't dare venture onto the dance floor again for the rest of the evening.

The following day passed slowly as I worried about

facing those fantastic young people in seminary on Monday morning. I had so many questions — Why? Why? Why?

Monday morning at 6:00 A.M. found me frantically floundering through my files! And then it hit me — a handout! (You know how exciting those handouts can be — right?) Why not put yourself in that classroom and complete the handout they received.

NO NAME, PLEASE

Question: What is your honest feeling about dancing the drape, or the "bear hug"?

_____

_____

_____

_____

Where on this continuum would you place yourself in regard to the way you feel you *should* dance? (Indicate with an X)

Where on this continuum would you place yourself in regard to the way you *do* dance? (Indicate with an O)

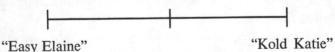

"Easy Elaine"   "Kold Katie"

Remember this:

To conform and be average is to be as near the bottom as the top!

Love,

Bro. Yorg

As this handout was discussed in class, it was apparent that there was a wide variety of feelings about this manner of dancing. Several of the comments were as follows:

"I didn't know there was anything wrong with it."

"I didn't know how to dance any other way."

"Everyone else did it, and you have to dance like that or guys won't ask you to dance."

"It's groovy, man!"

"I hate it, but I would rather do the bear hug than not dance at all!"

"Brother Yorgason, you are making such a big thing over something that isn't important at all."

"It depends on what your feelings are towards the boy. If you like him it's fine, although some boys about break your back."

"If you've danced ballroom dancing before, it's a blast. I really don't care for the drape because I get the feeling that sometimes guys get a little out of hand. If I get to feeling like a loaf of Wonder Bread (squeeze for freshness), I just step back and walk away."

"I like to dance that way because it doesn't look old-fashioned."

"I think it's stupid. I can't see how anyone can call it dancing. All you do is shuffle your feet and act like you are hanging on for dear life. It's so much fun to try dancing skills like waltz, fox trot, or swing. Even if you really like the guy, you still shouldn't bear hug because you shouldn't have different standards for different guys."

Perhaps the most unique response came from a young lady who went to the dance with a "mover." She had decided some time before that she wasn't going to dance the bear hug, and so as he put the moves on her, she stepped back and fearlessly said, "My body is a temple, not a visitors center, and you don't have a recommend!" That was perfect!

93

We discussed some alternatives, which are listed below.

1. Dance the drape, or the bear hug.
2. Refuse to dance at all, since you would rather not dance than to dance the bear hug.
3. Dance the conventional way — teach your partner.
4. Dance in the closed position. You can do this by not hanging on, but politely setting the girl's hands on the boy's shoulders with the boy putting his hands on the girl's waist.

Would you like my two cents worth? I told my students that alternatives three and four were the ones most acceptable in terms of adhering to Church standards. Dancing in the conventional manner is not a cure-all for dancing appropriately, but on the other hand, it is enjoyable and fun because it has so many variations. I challenged my students to try conventional dancing for one evening (the Sweetheart Ball was scheduled for the following Friday night). They accepted the challenge — for one evening only!

As they entered the dance that Saturday night, they grouped together and began dancing in the conventional open position. Before long others joined in, and by the time the evening was over, the dance floor was divided into two groups; those who were dancing conventionally and those who were intimately dancing the bear hug. As Monday morning rolled around, they could hardly contain themselves as they boasted of the fun they had dancing "my" way.

It should be pointed out that alternative number four is also acceptable. A couple does not have to melt together to enjoy dancing. Coincidentally, the couples that display their affection publicly, and have merely a physical relationship, find their romances rocky. Those who are more casual, or who are not caught up with only the physical part of their relationship, are those with deeper and more stable relationships.

94

As you develop relationships with the opposite sex, you are no doubt bombarded with all types of ideas pertaining to expressing physical affection. You want to feel good about yourself and you want to have the same feelings of respect for your partner.

In my opinion there are only three levels of affection which are acceptable as you prepare for temple marriage. These include a good-night kiss, several kisses during an evening, and light hugging and kissing which does not become too involved.

If this is our standard, why do so many young people take liberties which are not theirs to take? I really believe that young people actually develop appetites for physical affection. That is, when you first begin to date and interact with someone on a romantic basis, you are not aware of the physical options with your partner. In fact, you feel quite uncomfortable about any physical contact at all. As you continue to date, you become accustomed to each other, and then begin to express the feelings you have. As you become physically involved, you develop a desire or an appetite for affection.

There are several crucial factors which contribute to sexual appetite growth. K. Hardy points out some of them. They begin with early dating, where physical contact is permitted and even encouraged. When you begin to date early in life, you become used to your partner, and soon adopt the dating patterns your older brothers and sisters are experiencing.

Early dating leads to going steady early in your courtship years. When a young couple does this, they usually develop a dating pattern which is characterized by chronic love-making, or making out. No matter what your intentions are, if you date often enough and long enough, you will find that your relationship will gradually become primarily a physical one. Your parents realize this, so they naturally resist what you are doing.

95

Once you begin to center your relationship around physical intimacies, your mind becomes aware of negatively stimulating materials such as suggestive or obscene literature and sex-oriented motion pictures. When your minds are constantly infiltrated with these scenes and ideas, your appetite for these things continues to grow. You are undoubtedly aware of many who have little but sex on their minds. They may think they know "where it's at," but in reality they are being led down the path of spiritual destruction. If this continues, it is only a matter of time until they lower their moral standards. (K. Hardy, "An Appetitional Theory of Sexual Motivation," *Psychological Review,* 1964, pp. 1-17.)

As two people begin a romantic relationship, they tend to build it through intimacy and commitment. Before I explain this to you, spend a few moments looking at the accompanying illustration titled "Double Funnel Theory of Commitment and Intimacy."

As you study these funnels, you will see that as a couple travels down the funnels, they begin to feel an obligation to their dating partner to conform to the others' expectations. By giving and taking in each of the funnels, they progress down both of them. The boy allows himself to become committed, and in turn expects physical privileges from the girl.

The boy usually controls the commitment funnel because he is least committed in the relationship. The girl seeks for commitment and so the boy dictates how committed they become.

On the other hand, the girl usually controls the intimacy funnel. This occurs because the boy usually seeks for increased intimacy, and so the girl dictates just how far they go in their physical intimacies.

As you can see, the funnel becomes steeper as it goes down. When you are in the upper portion of the funnel, you have sure footing and are able to control the emotions you have. As you progress down the funnel, however, you

Double Funnel Theory of Commitment and Intimacy

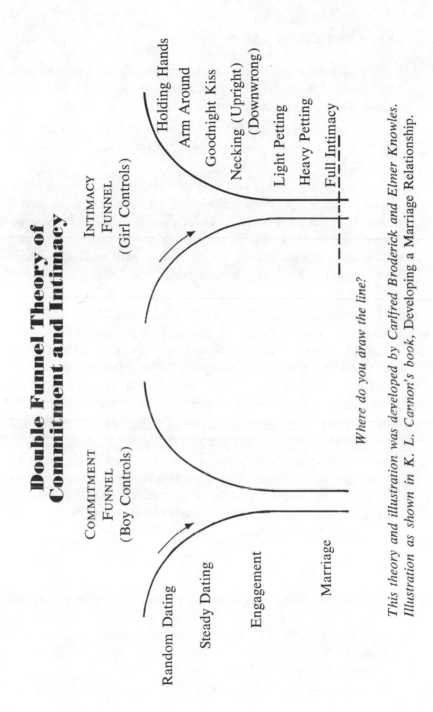

COMMITMENT
FUNNEL
(Boy Controls)

INTIMACY
FUNNEL
(Girl Controls)

Random Dating

Steady Dating

Engagement

Marriage

Holding Hands

Arm Around

Goodnight Kiss

Necking (Upright)
(Downwrong)

Light Petting

Heavy Petting

Full Intimacy

Where do you draw the line?

This theory and illustration was developed by Carlfred Broderick and Elmer Knowles.
Illustration as shown in K. L. Cannon's book, Developing a Marriage Relationship.

will find yourselves losing control of your emotions, and you will slide at a progressively accelerated pace until you have completely surrendered your virtue.

If you find yourself falling in the funnel, you have essentially three choices relating to your future and the future of your relationship.

First, by repenting you can climb back out and maintain your relationship. Even though this choice is the most desirable, it is the least logical. Once they have slipped into the steep sector, it is almost impossible for a couple to climb back out of the funnel together and still maintain their relationship. You may have a hard time believing this, but it is true!

Your second choice is to continue to wallow around in the steep sector, eventually hating yourself as well as your partner. Many young couples choose this alternative, which may lead to a loss of testimony, an unexpected pregnancy, and possibly an unstable and, more often than not, temporary marriage. This choice becomes a literal "hell."

A final alternative would be to break out of the funnel by dissolving your relationship with your partner. This is (in the short run) the hardest choice to make. In the long run, however, it is the only logical and safe choice you can make. I can promise you that if you exercise this option and fully repent, you can once again become clean in the sight of our Heavenly Father.

Becoming Clean Again

Do you fully understand the principle of repentance? You have probably listened to fifty lessons on this subject in your lifetime, yet some of you may want to know just what a person must do to receive complete forgiveness for something he may have done.

President David O. McKay once said this:

"Every principle and ordinance of the gospel of Jesus Christ is significant and important in contributing to the progress, happiness, and eternal life of man; but there is none more essential to the salvation of the human family than the divine and eternally operative principle of repentance. Without it, no one can be saved. Without it, no one can even progress." (*Improvement Era,* November 1968, p. 74.)

Some members of the Church have the idea that they can commit a sin and repent of it on a weekly basis. As long as they have a sin-free Saturday, they feel worthy to take the sacrament on Sunday. This is not true repentance.

As I was growing up, I had a friend who was deeply involved in a relationship with a girl, and would afford himself many privileges which weren't his to have. He would be intimate with his girl friend during the week but not on Saturdays, knowing he had to feel "worthy enough" to bless the sacrament on Sunday mornings. He later realized that he was merely deceiving himself and heaping condemnation upon himself by doing this. He later broke up with his girl, truly repented, and served an honorable mission.

99

Even though repentance is discussed a great deal, almost without exception those young people who come to me seeking direction ask, "How do we go about repenting?" For this reason, I thought it worthwhile to indicate a step-by-step program which, if followed, will allow you to once again be free from sin, and to be forgiven by our Heavenly Father.

Realize — Be aware that you have made a mistake and have really committed a sin.

Regret — Feel deeply sorry inside for what you have done.

Resolve — Make a firm and unwavering decision to change your ways.

Recite — Confess or admit your sins openly to (a) yourself, (b) the person you have sinned against, (c) your bishop, and (d) our Heavenly Father.

Reform — Forsake or discontinue any wrong behavior.

Repay — Make all possible repair of the damage your sin caused.

Release — Forgive others who have sinned. Hold no grudges.

Receive — Accept the gift of forgiveness from others and from our Heavenly Father.

Two steps mentioned here are perhaps harder to comply with than the others. Step number three is the first of these. Once you become laden with sin (and especially moral sin), it is very hard to resolve to make a change. This is because you have developed a habit, and habits can be very hard to break. It is also difficult because you are caught in a relationship which has some definite rewards.

It is most difficult to consider not going with someone you feel you love. Added to this problem is the fact that **100** because you are unclean, the Spirit of the Lord is not with you on a constant basis to assist you in overcoming the problems you are having. I often tell young people in this predicament that there are two ways to cut off a dog's tail — piece by piece, or all at once. Obviously, the least painful way to discontinue a losing relationship is to cut it off all at once, knowing you will have deep withdrawal pains, but knowing also that this is the most realistic way to repent and be forgiven.

A second step which is most difficult to take is that of confession. I think this is true because it is so often misunderstood. Here are the questions most often asked, together with my responses.

When should I confess?

Many people mull this question over and over in their minds, thinking that time will heal the situation and they won't have to confess. There is no time like the present. Before you do take this step, however, make a resolve that you are truly going to repent.

To whom should I confess?

Your personal repentance program should be a very private experience. The only ones who need to know are the person you have sinned against, your bishop or branch president, and our Heavenly Father.

Why is it necessary to confess to my bishop?

This is a serious question in the minds of most young people. A bishop is responsible for you during the time you live in his ward. He has been given the keys of stewardship. There are two immediate results that stem from laying your problems before the bishop. First, by sharing your problem with him in confidence, you now have it off your own shoulders and you sense a feeling of relief which is essential as you seek to regain your self-worth and self-esteem. Second, when you share these things with your bishop, he can be used as a pillar to lean on, a stabilizer, a confidant who can not only see your situation more clearly than you, but who can assist you with counsel and encouragement as you climb out of the dilemma you are now in. Have faith in him. He is directed to keep your confidence, and your humility and desire to change will give him much respect and admiration for you.

101

What is the advantage of confessing?

It helps you to become free from the weight of that sin; to throw off the guilt feelings; to begin to feel good about yourself because you know you are being true to yourself and true to our Father in heaven.

Controlling Your Emotions

Now you have some facts in mind about repentance and forgiveness, but how can you control your thoughts and actions? From my notes taken from a lecture by L. Scoresby, let me bring the following suggestions.

Perhaps the best way to control your emotions in your dating years is to fill your life with gratifying experiences so that you don't resort to physical intimacies as an escape from boredom or emotional starvation. In other words, fill your dates with a variety of experiences (perferably with other couples) so you will not have the time or the desire to indulge in intimacies.

You should understand that, although it is vital and natural to have strong feelings of attraction toward the opposite sex, intimacies enhance a relationship only when you are married.

As you date, place confidence in each other, and emphasize the long-term rewards of remaining pure. These rewards include personal respect for each other, trust in your marriage, a solid foundation for your relationship, and, most importantly, the blessing of beginning your life together with the presence of our Father's Spirit in your home.

102

To be more specific, here are some ideas which can assist you as much as anything we have discussed. These ideas have provided young people with more ammunition in combating Satan than anything else I know. (L. Scoresby, Education Week Lecture.)

These ideas are presented as a formula which, if followed, will assist you and your partner as you strive to limit your display of affection for each other.

To introduce this formula to you, I will introduce two hypothetical young people who feel they have a relationship they would like to continue, and who are both mature enough to handle such a subject. Let's call them Scott and Micci. They begin by announcing that they want to have a talk. This is the first step, and can be taken by either partner. The best timing is to talk after you have had a good date, perhaps after Sunday dinner or after a fireside.

The second step is to tell your partner that you have some ideas you would like to share. You then define your nonverbal behavior. That is, you talk about what has been happening in your relationship that has not been verbally expressed. Scott handles it like this:

"What does it mean to you, Micci, when I put my arm around you?"

"It really makes me feel secure, Scott. I have a feeling that you really want and need me."

"Scott, there is one thing that is bothering me about our relationship."

"What's that, Micci?"

"Well, I don't feel right about how free we are with our kisses. I just think a kiss should be more special than we are making it."

"You know, Micci, I have been having similar feelings. I think our relationship is beginning to concentrate on the physical, and is crowding out personal growth as well as growth in our relationship."

103

Micci and Scott must now decide together the limits they would both feel comfortable with. In other words, how far out of the funnel should they remain? Each of them should have a say in the setting of these limits, and a certain degree of negotiating may take place until a definite agreement has been made. Perhaps the conversation would continue like this:

"Micci, you might think I am weird or something, but I really believe we should limit our kissing to a single good-night kiss."

"Do you really think we could honor that limit, Scott?"

"You know, honey, I think if we both decided, we could do anything we set our minds to."

"Scott, I really do appreciate you. So many of my girl friends have to fight boys off, and yet you want to honor your priesthood completely. Thank you for being you, Scott."

"I think you have to put credit where credit is due, Micci. I have you on such a high pedestal that I could never do anything to you. Is it settled then?"

"You bet! Let's shake on it!"

"Uh — oh — ah — yeh, let's do!"

The next thing to discuss in this conversation is a procedure for changing the limits you have set.

"You know, Scott, I would like to suggest that we have another talk like this in the future. What do you think?"

"I agree. Let's say in a month from now. We may feel differently about each other as our relationship progresses. Micci, I really believe we have something special, and I don't want to do anything that would detract from the spirit that is with us right now. By the way, if our feelings change before next month, I hope we are both mature enough to bring it up again."

The final area to consider in this conversation is what course to take if you violate the limits you have set. What happens to your relationship? Do you simply ignore a violation, or do you impose a penalty for doing so? Let's illustrate once again with Scott and Micci.

"I feel fine about what we have decided, Micci, but what happens if we pass the limits we have set?"

"Well, I have some feelings about that, dear, but I would like to hear what you have to say first."

"Well, I surely don't have all the answers, darling, but I feel like this. If we are going to have a marriage relationship, we have to build a strong foundation. It's my impression that before two people can love each other, they have to respect each other. Respect is not a variable, but is a constant in our feelings. Anyway, if we honestly respect ourselves then we can gain respect for each other. Once this respect is established, we can begin to build trust in our relationship. I don't want to sound stuffy, but if we aren't mature enough

People in this situation also lose the sense of trust that involves being able to predict that their partner will act in a warm, trusting manner. Married couples have made a commitment in public, but in a dating relationship there is little or no commitment, thus there is no assurance that the relationship will continue. If this loss of trust exists in a relationship before marriage, the chances are great that it will continue through the years of marriage.

Finally, the act of making love or procreation is perhaps the most powerful and profound experience two people can share, and after they have experienced it, they start to center their whole relationship around it.

Remember this: Love is *not* taking your partner where he or she does not want to go. (L. Scoresby, Education Week Lecture.)

108

FREE LOVE

Free love?
Yes — Isn't that what
has always made
love . . . love?
But unrestrained
gratification of
one's lusts —
Isn't it self-
control that
separates man
from animals?
Yes. Love is free.
Lust has an
ugly price.

— *Sallie Clinton*

When a partner in a relationship imposes himself upon you, this partner does not truly love you, but rather "lusts" you. When this happens, you become an object with which to satisfy lustful desires, and your relationship will last only as long as you give in to the desires of your partner. When you say no, and withdraw your affections, your partner will leave you and begin dating someone who also craves lust and physical intimacy.

The Very Key

Elder Boyd K. Packer of The Council of the Twelve has given some valuable insights into our purpose here upon the earth, our opportunity to become as God is through the power of free agency and by exercising correct choices. Here are some of the points he makes:

Two great things were in store for us as we came into mortality. First, we were given a mortal body through which by proper control we might receive eternal life and glory; and second, we were told that we would be tried and tested and thus gain strength to become like our Father in heaven.

109

As we left our pre-earthly existence, we were told that we would be receiving with our bodies the "very key" to progression and godhood — the power to procreate, to have children. This power to procreate would have at least two dimensions — it would be strong, and it would remain constant. It would need to be strong because rearing children is a difficult task, and many would be reluctant to have children if the built-in desires were not strong. In addition to this, the act itself serves as an expression of "oneness" between a husband and wife, and because it is constant, couples rely upon this experience as a vital spoke in their wheel of love. When a couple waits until they are married before expressing their love in this manner, they are allowing this expression to become much more than just physical. On the other hand, for young people who are subtly enticed into using these creative powers prematurely, the experience is shallow and unsatisfying at best.

So feel grateful that you experience these urgings, for they are indeed given to you by our Father. But give yourself one of the greatest of all gifts, the gift of self-mastery and personal righteousness.

The gravest consequence of premarital intimacy is the loss of the Holy Ghost in our lives. Our Heavenly Father really knows and understands each of us. He knows our needs and desires, and he understands our weaknesses. He has also promised us that if we will keep his commandments we will not become tempted beyond our personal ability to endure. (Boyd K. Packer, *The Very Key* [Salt Lake City: Published for Seminaries and Institutes].)

110

It is my sincere hope and prayer that you have understood the things presented in this chapter, and that you will use these pages as a point of reference. These things are true, and if you apply this knowledge in your dating relationships, you will find joy and satisfaction. Elder Paul H. Dunn has said that "our attitude determines our altitude." (Paul H. Dunn, Address to BYU 71st Branch, November 1972.) May you equip yourselves for battle, and may your attitude reflect the "on guard" position. Your reward will be evident as you enter the temple on "your" day, knowing you are both pure and worthy of each other. Give this gift to yourself!

Chapter 9

The Choice
Is Yours

It was not long ago that I was wondering with apprehensive anticipation just who I was going to marry. It was while completing my mission in Puerto Rico that I penned my thoughts about the girl of my dreams:

"April 28, 1966
San Juan, Puerto Rico

"Dear Dream Girl:

"There will be a time in an appointed place for an eternal reason that you and I will once again meet, to fulfill the measure of our creation. To this end I am now preparing.

"I say that we will meet again, because as you know, our hearts were one as we progressed in our premortal existence — and then in parting to take our mortal forms on this goodly habitation, we were promised that, in accordance with our righteous deeds and desires, we would be granted the most sacred opportunity and responsibility known to mankind: that of perpetuating our seed in rearing a number of our spiritual brothers and sisters as they leave the presence of our Creator.

"Now, Dream Girl, you are no doubt in wonderment as to why my thoughts and heart are turned to you, while I labor as a missionary on this far-away fertile island. You see, Dear One, it has been impressed so firmly on my mind that along with bringing joy to others, we missionaries should evaluate our lives so as to prepare for life with choice spirits such as you, thus making available the opportunity of eternal partnership with God, as we enter into his rest.

"I have often felt that although my missionary activity has given my heart more complete joy and satisfaction than any other previous experience in my life, there is still a corner of my heart which is left unexposed to life, left empty to be one day filled and consumed by a God-given gift — your love and sincere devotion.

"Is it then with any wonder, my love, that I address you at this time?

"Perhaps you may ask, 'How is it he knows it is me he at one time revered?' To this let me state:

112

"How is it a bird knows when to turn south, as the leaves turn to brown and to gold?

"How is it a lamb, being lost in a storm, can safely return to its fold?

"Or what turns in the heart of a man aged with sin, as he kneels now in meekness toward heaven?

"I'm sure it's the still, self-same power from on high. From our Maker it's surely been given.

"The prophet has said that I'll know who to marry, by the whispering of that still small voice.

"When I find a companion in whose presence I'm inspired, to grow and progress at my choice.

"During the past several months, I have encountered mistakes made in homes where the gospel's not been.

"And I'm grateful, Dream Girl, that it has charted my course — Yes, I've grown from the things I have seen.

"It is true there'll be times when problems we'll face, and Satan will seek to destroy.

"Yet, with the priesthood of God protecting our home —
Be assured it's true power we'll employ.

"Now, Dream Girl, continue pursuing the course; the
road that for us is appointed.

"Until we kneel in the temple of God, and are made 'one'
by the Lord's true anointed.

"This is my humble prayer and desire.

> "Preparing to be yours,
> "B.G.Y."

This letter was given to my dear Margaret almost two
years after, as we sat beneath the spires of the temple in
Salt Lake City. We had both served missions, had each
attended three years of college, and felt very ready to meet.
Just eighteen hours before we met, I knelt at my bedside and
expressed my feelings to our Father. I indicated to him that
evening that I felt my life was in order, that I had experience
enough to know what I did and did not need in a companion;
and then I left the matter in his hands. I promised him that
I would be sensitive to his Spirit as he guided me in this most
crucial choice. This was accomplished, and as I met my wife
the spirit bore witness that she was the one. Although we
said only a few things to each other, I ran home from Sunday
School exclaiming to my parents that I had met my wife!
I thought that this was the beginning of the end, and yet
I have come to appreciate since that day that it was simply
the end of the beginning.

Factors to Consider

Many of you may have a spiritual experience similar to
the one mentioned above. If you follow true to national
statistics, 93 percent of you will marry. As you prepare for
this blessing, you will have many things to consider. Perhaps
you have asked yourself, "How does one go about selecting
a mate?"

113

There are several ideas about selecting a mate that may be of interest to you. Before going into these, the idea (mentioned in the letter) about knowing our mates even in the pre-existence should be put into perspective. Although this is possible, for most of us it is not likely. It is my opinion that each of you develops personality traits which cause you to become unique. Because of what or who you have become, you will select a companion you feel comfortable with, one you feel will bring you happiness and satisfaction. There are probably many people you could feel compatible and happy with, rather than just one.

Many ideas are floating around which try to explain how to go about selecting your mate. Many feel that you are attracted to, and marry, the person with whom you share similar characteristics. As was mentioned earlier, there are those who feel that you will marry one who has the greatest possibility of satisfying your needs, and whose needs you can also satisfy.

114

As I was formulating in my mind the type of person I would marry, it was very important to me to select someone whose strengths complemented my weaknesses, and vice versa. My reasoning was that we could assist each other in overcoming and "becoming." Incidentally, this has proven to be the case in our relationship, and has helped both of us to grow and improve as individuals.

While the ideas mentioned above are not conclusive, perhaps they have given you an idea of what to consider when selecting your mate.

What Do You Share?

As you begin to develop relationships which may lead to marriage, there are several things to keep in mind.

It is vital that you share interests which are important to each of you. It is sad to note that almost daily young people

marry without really getting to know each other, thinking that all will be heaven with only roses along the path. Because they do not take time to share in each other's interests, they have no way of knowing how compatible they will be with each other. The couple that shares no (or few) common interests will have only temporary excitement in their marriage.

Should you find yourself in a relationship you question because of this, it would be well to level with your companion, and discuss your concern. A positive alternative to breaking up would be for each of you to make a conscious effort to learn about the other's likes and dislikes, and try to find more common interests.

You should seek the association of those with whom you share the same values and ideals. The apostle Paul said, "Be ye not unequally yoked together with unbelievers." (2 Corinthians 6:14.)

116

To help you know if you are compatible, why not explore many different aspects of your lives? All too often, courtship activities center around commercial entertainment. This could be a crucial mistake for any couple! Initially, it is easier to constantly be entertained, but in the long run you would be cheating yourselves.

Allow your association with each other to be more of a casual day-to-day sharing of common activities. This might include baking together, washing each other's cars together, hiking, hunting, walking, washing dishes, and simply talking. This dating approach eventually exposes your true character and interests to each other, and thus enables each to see how compatible his partner really is.

The type of interaction that allows you to see your partner (and your partner to see you) in crisis or stress situations is also important. I will never forget that a good friend of mine had her marriage break up after only two weeks of marriage because her husband had been dishonest with her.

She had known him for such a short time that she did not know when he wasn't being truthful.

It was discussed in the dating chapter that social experiences are ofttimes just guessing games. Many times a person will "put on" or pretend to be someone or something he's not, and often he can fool his partner for quite some time. For this reason, you should never lock yourself into a relationship until it has withstood the test of time. It is very easy (when caught up in the ecstasy of love) to want to get married "right now" rather than wait and test the feelings you have for each other. There is no reason to marry in a hurry when eternity hangs in the balance!

Despite these good reasons for waiting, many couples marry in a hurry. They cannot wait to selfishly satisfy the physical desires they have for each other. If your relationship is a mature one, you will see the wisdom in waiting. You may be too involved to see the danger signals, but warnings usually come from your parents or those who are closest to your relationship. Don't ever let your pride stop you from accepting counsel and help from those who love you most. Just be grateful for this guidance! If your parents have reservations about your marriage, why not test those reservations?

117

President David O. McKay said this: "Under such circumstances, no matter how fascinated you may be, young woman, no matter how confident you may feel that you love him, let your judgment rule and you be master of your feelings. It may grieve you not to follow the inclination of your heart, but you had better be pained a little in your youth than to suffer pangs of torture later." (David O. McKay, *Instructor,* July 1965, p. 258.)

One of the most important aspects of your relationship is what you do for each other. Do you find that many of your dates end with one or both of you in tears? Do you find that you are not a better person when you are associating with your companion? Do your standards become difficult to maintain? For true happiness, it is essential that a relationship be one in which each partner is inspired to be a better person. If you do not bring out the best in your partner, or vice versa, you had better (for both your sakes) climb out now before you have three or four children and find that you have no marriage after all.

One of my saddest experiences was to sit in my office and listen as a student explained how she and her boy friend were going to elope. Both sets of parents disagreed with the relationship, as did most of the young couple's friends. This girl admitted that she didn't love her boy friend, but she felt she should marry him because of the intimacies they had shared. She could not imagine sharing herself with any other man, and so she was willing to forsake all counsel and marry someone she didn't love. She did marry him, but after one child they are now separated, awaiting a divorce.

118

It is most important when you develop meaningful relationships to be in a position to take advantage of the greatest resource available to you — your Heavenly Father. He knows each one of you personally, and has provided his Spirit to guide and assist you at this most crucial time.

Sometimes it seems particularly difficult for you young ladies, as you may wonder if you will have more than one chance to marry. Many young ladies accept a proposal for this reason alone, justifying it to themselves on the grounds that they would rather have a small slice of the pie than no pie at all. Following this reasoning will bring only heartache and misery in the future. Set your sights high, and with the help of our Father you will hit exactly what you are aiming at.

Chapter 10

Guess What, Folks? We're Engaged!

For most of you this expression is used but once; others may experience several such occasions. It might surprise you to know that between 30 and 40 percent of all engaged couples break up. This chapter will explore the purposes of this unique time period as well as the frustrations which may appear.

Today the engagement is viewed as a mutual pledge between partners to marry. Although this commitment should be entered into only after the relationship has developed sufficiently, it does not absolutely require that the partners marry each other.

There are a number of good reasons for having an engagement period. K. L. Cannon suggests four as follows:

1. It is a time for testing the relationship.
2. It is a transition period.
3. It is used in developing a mutual dependence.
4. It is a time for preparation and planning.

(Cannon, *Developing a Marriage Relationship,* pp. 222-225.)

Testing the relationship. Prior to an engagement there exists a more insecure, informal relationship. Because there has been little or no commitment made, uncertainty may exist in the mind of at least one of the partners. When a couple formally agrees to marry, they have a sense of obligation to themselves and to their partner to be open and candid about their feelings.

Following the announcement that they are engaged, a couple should make a conscious effort to honestly test their relationship to determine its depth and solidarity. One of the most crucial tests you can give yourselves is that of value compatibility. Your values cannot be changed simply by saying they will be. Even after marriage you are still individuals, and if you truly desire satisfaction in your marriage, you will have to understand and be able to accept the values and ideas each of you have.

To assist you in this quest, I have included a set of questions for you to consider. As you complete this checklist, do so openly and honestly. Do not attempt to mask your true feelings, because masks are very damaging to a marriage.

120

TESTING YOUR ENGAGEMENT

Yes No 1. Have you visited in each other's homes to the point of recognizing that normal family behavior is practiced even though the prospective in-laws are there?

Yes No 2. Has each of you become well enough acquainted with the other's friends that you are clear about your attitudes toward them?

Yes No 3. Have you seen each other in a crisis, or under tension, or at a time when strong feelings were involved?

Yes No 4. Have you checked financial costs by actually looking at living quarters, shopping together, and by pricing and examining furniture?

Yes No 5. Cooperatively, and through open discussion, have you arrived at premarital sex standards acceptable to each?

Yes No 6. Do you feel free and relaxed in expressions of affection?

Yes No 7. Have you from time to time enjoyed being together when you were not occupied with doing something or being with other people?

Yes No 8. Have you been in situations where you had to work together as a team, such as caring for children, entertaining your families or friends, or working on a committee?

Yes No 9. Have you worked through some definite differences of opinion in a manner satisfactory to both of you?

Yes No 10. Is your fiance(e) able and willing to accept you as you are?

121

Yes No 11. Are you able and willing to accept your fiance(e) as he (she) is?

Yes No 12. Have you spent a prolonged time together when each had to be his honest and unadorned self?

13. Have you discussed in detail your ideas on:
   Yes No Discipline of children?
   Yes No When to have children?
   Yes No Future relations with each other's families?
   Yes No Use of contraceptives?
   Yes No Additional attitudes towards sex in marriage?
   Yes No Feelings toward each other's friends?
   Yes No Attitudes toward religious practices and church attendance?
   Yes No Attitudes toward your initial sex experiences?

Transition period. Until this time you have probably been most concerned with what you want and with what is best for you. It is now critical that you begin to look away from yourself and concern yourself with what is best for both of you. You will start to make the transition from "I" and "me" to "we" and "us."

Developing a mutual dependence. It is not a weakness to become dependent upon each other in your relationship. Those couples who want to maintain individual independence are losing sight of what marriage is all about. Not long ago, I read a poem that had been the motto of a fellow who had just divorced his wife. It said that each of them should be totally his own person, "do his own thing" and not plan to live up to the other's expectations. Can you imagine adopting this as the motto of your marriage? It is a doctrine that will destroy a marriage. We should try to live up to each other's expectations. After all, marriage is living our lives together. Those who leave happiness and unity to chance greatly increase their chances of never finding it.

Preparation and planning. Someone once said that when the time for performance presents itself the time for preparation is past.

You have been subconsciously preparing for marriage since you were a child. You have learned much from the structure and functioning of your family. Your social experiences outside the home have also been a general preparation for you, especially in interacting with those of the opposite sex. The engagement period is the time for specifics.

There are several things about marriage that require a good deal of planning. One of the first items to consider is finances. Few areas of consideration are more important than this. If you marry without "thought for tomorrow," you will most likely have no tomorrow together.

As I came home from my mission, I considered the importance of wise use of money and made some decisions.

122

For one thing, I decided that I would buy nothing on credit; that I would purchase something only if I had saved enough money to do so. This policy was later modified to allow debt only for an automobile and a home. Now, nine years later, the only debt we will allow is a mortgage on our home.

Along with this debt-free program, I decided to have separate savings accounts for various purposes. Therefore, I opened a "diamond ring" account. I saved enough money so that when we became engaged, the ring was purchased without incurring a debt. Incidentally, that account was then changed to a "baby" account. In the birth of our four sons, when we have incurred expenses not covered by insurance, this account has adequately provided.

We now have seven separate saving accounts, five of which are for our sons' missions. We have only four children, but our philosophy dictates that we have an account for our next child. If that child is a girl (we can hope, can't we?) the savings account will pay for her wedding expenses.

123

Can you see how prior planning has assisted us? We also have one savings account in which we always maintain a thousand-dollar balance. This is our emergency account, which we use for anything unplanned, always paying ourselves back *with interest*. We live in a society where charging and financing has become a way of life, and so many marriages are burdened with debt. This is in direct contrast to the counsel members of the Church have received from the prophet to maintain a debt-free financial posture. I can tell you from experience how great it is never to have had a family argument because we were feeling financial pressure. All it takes is making up your minds. We have found that it is just as easy to live your life a thousand dollars ahead as it is to live it a thousand dollars in the red. In fact, it is really easier.

As an engaged couple, you should have conversations about income, means of livelihood, the type of apartment or home that will be suitable, transportation, and household possessions. You may find that you simply cannot afford to marry at present, or you may decide to alter your expectations so that you can marry. Don't set your standard of living so high before marriage that you find yourself in the position of those described in this poem:

> The bride, white of hair,
> Stooped over her cane,
> Her footsteps needed guiding;
> While down the church aisle
> With a wan, toothless smile
> The groom in his wheelchair came riding.
> And who is that elderly couple thus wed?
> You'll find when you've closely explored it,
> That this is that rare,
> Most conservative pair,
> Who waited till they could afford it!
>
> — *Author unidentified*

124

As you progress in your engagement, you will find that your relationship is either weakening or becoming stronger and more vital. Perhaps some danger signals will help you recognize if you have a losing relationship.

Danger Signals

In their book, *Building a Successful Marriage,* Landis and Landis point out that in most marriages that fail, especially those that fail early, there were danger signals which, if recognized by the couple during dating and courtship, would have warned them against trying to form a permanent relationship with each other.

Giving yourself time enough for recognizing danger signals is essential. Couples who short-circuit the dating phase and marry after brief acquaintance block the possibility of such warnings becoming clear during courtship. Some of the most common of these warnings are:

1. Frequent and regular lovers' quarrels. It is true that a few quarrels may occur in potentially good relationships, but if, over a period of time, quarrels continue to occur, one should evaluate the quarrels objectively. Do they have a pattern? Do certain types of events or situations tend to result in a quarrel? If the engagement period is characterized by quarreling, marriage will likely be that way too.

2. Breaking up, and doubts. It is a danger signal if couples break up and make up again once or more during their dating. Even if they do not break up, but only consider it, or if one, especially the girl, has doubts about their relationship, something is likely to be wrong. All the findings indicate that the girl, her family, and her friends are more accurate in judging danger signals in relationships.

There is a very high association between premarital confidence in the future of the relationship and later marital happiness.

A certain measure of hesitancy is natural for any thoughtful person making a lifetime (and eternal) decision. The individual can test his doubts by comparing his feelings about this matter with his way of approaching decisions on other matters. If he has doubts, and his family and friends have doubts, there is likely to be a sound basis for the attitudes.

3. A strong desire to change the other person. A strong basic respect for each other is very important. A desire to change the other person means a less than complete acceptance of this person as he or she is, and it is likely that the two could not meet each other's needs without more changing than would be possible. Basic personality structure is fairly well set by the time of marriage; it will be difficult even to change oneself much after that, and quite impossible to change another person.

A sincere respect for the mate's ideals and goals in life and for each other's moral standard is also necessary.

4. Does the relationship bring out the best in the indi-

vidual? A satisfying courtship should bring out the best in both partners. For the courtship period to be characterized by feelings of depression and moodiness in one who is fairly content and cheerful means there is danger ahead.

5. Others. Matters that both tactfully avoid discussing, or that either "blocks" on, are the ones that should be given more serious, objective thought.

Differences about friends may be significant. A difference over friends may indicate other basic differences in points of view and in goals in life. (J. T. Landis and M. G. Landis, *Building a Successful Marriage* [New Jersey: Prentice-Hall, 1963].)

Do You Have Doubts?

This subject was touched on previously, but it will be useful to take a closer look at the doubts which occur during the engagement period.

126

Many young people experience a relatively crisis-free dating experience; that is, until they become engaged. Suddenly their whole relationship changes, and they find themselves at each other's throats constantly. They may find that their relationship is not as natural or spontaneous as it was before becoming engaged. They may even find that rather than feeling secure, they feel "locked in" and confined as a person. Many new factors enter into a relationship when a couple becomes engaged.

All (or almost all) engagements are laced with doubts of one sort or another. You must remember that the doubts are not important, but the basis for the doubts is important. A person may have doubts about himself, about his partner, or about the relationship in general. These doubts may be situational, and would be removed if something changed. They are valid, yet not nearly as crucial as doubts which are personal.

As doubts arise, they must not be camouflaged or passed over, but should be considered openly by the persons involved.

If doubts exist, you should seek guidance from someone in whom you can confide. You need not be afraid of a confidant's reaction as you share these doubts with him. Most likely he will only want to help you resolve your doubts the best way possible.

Is It Right to Call It Off?

It is not only right, but it is totally justified if there are proper reasons. In our culture there is a great deal of pressure to become engaged in preparation for an eternal relationship. Because of this, engagement often occurs when the couple has reached a level of maturity beyond the norms of our society. This has a disadvantage in that the persons becoming engaged sense that they must live "up to" their understanding of others' expectations of their maturity.

Related to this frustration is the question so often posed by couples as they struggle to free themselves from their relationship. "How can we break our engagement when we felt that the Lord directed us to become engaged in the first place?"

127

This was the question asked by a very close friend not long ago. He and his partner had become engaged after a relatively short dating relationship, and did so on the basis of having received an answer to their prayers. After becoming engaged, they found themselves in the midst of many conflicts. Unable to maintain their moral standards, and realizing that they were no longer worthy to enter the temple for their marriage, they had the date postponed. Gradually their relationship weakened until it was finally terminated by mutual agreement.

There are several things to consider when such a serious decision is needed, especially if a couple feels that their engagement was an answer to prayer. Many times young people are so caught up in the emotions of love that they spend only five minutes on their knees, then arise and answer their own prayers. There is a fine line between our own emotions and the whisperings of the Spirit of the Lord. I have found that an effective way to determine the source of my feelings is to test those feelings with time. When a person answers his own prayers (and the answer is not in this person's best interest), his feelings will usually follow a "roller coaster" pattern. That is, they will be up (very positive) one day and the next day will be down (filled with doubts and uncertainties). This is just opposite from receiving confirmation from the Spirit. Feelings that are so confirmed remain constant and firm.

Perhaps you need to define your feelings as well as your relationship. I believe there are two types of relationships, those that are upward thrusting and those that are downward spiraling. The upward thrusting relationships are built upon trust and respect, then real love. These relationships reflect happiness and satisfaction, with concrete shared goals and ambitions. In this type of relationship there is no way that either partner would violate the other's virtue. These couples recognize the emotions they have for each other, yet because they are directed by the Spirit of the Lord, they involve themselves in wholesome activities so that they will not be tempted.

A final thought about why feelings change after a couple receives an answer to prayer has to do with the reason behind the spiritual impression they received. It is my opinion that at certain times in our lives our Heavenly Father sees that a need we may have can be filled in a given relationship. He therefore allows us to feel secure in our relationship "for a period of time" so that our particular needs can be fulfilled. This is not realized by the couple at the time, yet in reflecting upon these deep relationships, the wisdom of going with that person is usually realized and appreciated.

These ideas are intended only as a guide for you at a critical time in your lives. Remember, it is not a disgrace to

break an engagement if your motives and reasons are sound. It is best to mutually terminate a relationship, so that the egos are left intact. If you have to call it off without your partner's consent, do so tactfully. This is most easily done by being critical of your relationship rather than of your partner. Your feelings have changed, but keep in mind that your partner is sensitive and has feelings too, and may eventually become engaged and marry someone else. You can show leadership by building the partner even though you are breaking up. Nothing is accomplished by burning bridges as you leave a relationship.

Make the Engagement Period Enjoyable

We have spent a good bit of time discussing relationships that are eventually terminated. This will serve only as information for most of you. In most cases, the engagement period is a happy and exciting time. It should be a peaceful time too, as you are preparing to be husband and wife, and your love is building and growing. You will have many tasks in preparing for marriage, but take the time to enjoy yourselves. Get involved in activities that bring out your personality and provide opportunities for interacting with each other.

What is the proper length of this engagement period? I personally feel that three to four months is just right. This much time allows you to make the necessary preparations. It also provides enough time to test your relationship and to explore your personalities. If you are together constantly and have an engagement that lasts longer than this, you probably will cause yourselves frustrations and concern. As your love grows, and as you become more intimately acquainted, you will want to express the feelings you are having. You know that you want to remain worthy, so frustration occurs. It is not fair for either of you to have this happen. On the one hand, it is good for you to learn to control your emotions; but on the other hand, your physical relationship should progress at a steady pace with the other areas of your relationship, always within the proper bounds. This is why too much too quickly will only impair your chances of survival in the long run, while too long an engagement will tend to impose an unreasonable burden of restraint.

May this time be one of excitement and anticipation for you, and may you make the effort to become dependent upon each other and to make good use of the time you are together.

131

Chapter 11

The Perfect Date

The clock clicked its warning, but before it could sound its alarm, Dave quickly released the knob and sat upright. It was still dark outside, and a light rain could be heard falling on the sycamore leaves. Without thinking, he tossed back the covers and pulled the small Indian rug over to the bed. "I'm going to miss this old rug," he thought to himself; and then with conviction his body swung down and he began to pray.

"Dear Father, so much has happened to me these past few weeks that I hardly know where to begin. . . ."

Dave brushed back a tear as he arose from his knees. "Boy, have I got to hurry," he thought as he bounded into the shower. "It's straight-edge time this morning. Can't rely on Norelco this time, ol' man!"

Upstairs, Dave could hear the rest of the family; all up for his day. "They'd better be hustling," he thought, as he glanced down at his watch. "Now where could I have put my shoe horn? I bet Kelly carried it off. Flip!

"Oh, wow! I've got to be one lucky guy! I wonder what she's doing right now. Sure hope she'll be ready, 'cause this is one date we can't be late for!

"You've got to stop talking to that mirror, Dave! She'd flip her lid if she found out."

As Suzanne peered through the drapes she thought she could see a break in the clouds. It was beginning to get light, and she had already been up for an hour.

"Only thirty-five minutes," she sang as she pressed the toothpaste onto the brush. "I wonder if Dave squeezes it from the bottom or the middle," she thought. "It's got to be the middle; otherwise, we wouldn't have a perfect beginning for our marriage."

Rinsing her mouth, Suzanne caught a glimpse at her roommate standing in the hall. "Are you sure you want to go through with it, Suzie? Just say the word and I'll be happy to take your place!"

"Ann, I'm so happy! I never thought this day would arrive, and now that it's here I hardly know where to begin. Could you please get my dress from the wardrobe and hang it on the front door? It would be just like me to walk off and forget the most important thing."

Her stomach was growling again. "I'm so nervous," she thought as she began to blow her hair. "Dave is wise to think we should fast this morning. And to think that in just three more hours I will be Mrs. David Edgar Hall. Oh, I just hope he likes my hair."

Suzanne's heart leaped as the doorbell rang. "Two minutes early," she muttered as she slipped into her shoes.

"Come in!" someone yelled as she rounded the corner from the bedroom. The door opened wide, and there, all smiles, was Dave!

"Good morning! This is the happiest guy in the world here to escort the most beautiful girl in the world to the most heavenly place in the world. May I come in?"

Even while he was talking, Suzanne zipped up her suitcase and lifted her dress from the knob. "Good morning, my handsome prince! Shall we be on our way?"

"Well — ah — the folks are in the car waiting. How

133

about letting me kiss my fiancee good-morning? I won't have the chance to kiss an unmarried lady too many more times, you know."

The '66 Chevy seemed to float down the road on that drizzly morning. As they passed through Mt. Pleasant, Dave pointed excitedly at the doctor's office in which he was born. They drove through the blinking light and on to Ephraim. They could now see the temple as it loomed majestically in the distance, appearing almost suspended in the air.

Up close the spires glistened. The clouds were breaking now, and sun was just beginning to peer through the trees to the east. Several seagulls floated overhead as Dave and Suzanne entered through the north door.

134   Once inside, an attendant asked to see their recommends. Dave beamed as he pulled them both from his wallet. He recalled how he had put them there for safekeeping as they left the stake president's office. Suzanne smiled too, as she reflected back on that moment. She had given him her recommend — just to give him that needed feeling. Now she was glad that she had.

They walked up the stairs where they were asked to remove their shoes. "This temple is even more beautiful than I had imagined," Suzanne mused as they walked into the chapel. The rest of the family were seated toward the front, and so, without saying a word to each other, they parted and sat with their parents.

After a few moments they were escorted to their dressing rooms, where they dressed in their sacred temple clothing. Dave had suggested that the visitors too should dress in white so that this special occasion would be remembered that way.

After dressing, they were all taken upstairs. Suzanne could hardly contain herself as she whispered to Dave, "You know what? My heart is just pounding! Dear, I want to come

back often so that we can keep these memories fresh in our minds."

"Suzanne, I have never felt the Spirit of the Lord so strongly. It may sound trite, but I want you by my side forever. Shhhh — I think it's our turn."

It was almost like heaven as everyone passed into the blue sealing room. It was in this same room that both Dave's and Suzanne's parents and grandparents had been married. Knowing this, they felt that no other sealing room would be quite so perfect.

Each listened intently to the counsel given by the temple president. As they looked across the room, they could see their reflection in the facing mirrors repeated again and again, as though they were looking into eternity.

136

After a few moments the temple president invited them to stand. Dave was then asked to assist Suzanne to kneel at the holy marriage altar. Returning to the other side, Dave knelt and took Suzanne's hand, and under the authority of the priesthood they were made "one" — for time and for all eternity.

Each day this dream is re-enacted throughout the world after special young people like yourselves accept the challenge to *become* the right one.

Nothing in this world is more sacred and beautiful, unless it is the culmination of this experience — creating life. As your date draws near, you will come to appreciate that the excitement, the peace, and the contentment are indescribable.

It is difficult for me to understand how two young people who have been taught the true and eternal perspective of the temple could marry for time only, thereby denying themselves all of the blessings and insights which accompany a temple wedding. Each of you is truly a unique person, and you deserve the birthright you have been given.

In speaking about eternal marriage, President Spencer W. Kimball had this to say:

"Our young people are wonderful, with rich and glorious promises. The Lord loves you, we love you, and we want you to do right and enjoy the blessings and happiness that come with righteous living.

"We have confidence in you and promise you rich blessings and a happy life if you listen and study and pray and keep your life totally directed along the straight and narrow way outlined by our Lord, Jesus Christ." (Spencer W. Kimball, Address to Youth, Salt Lake City, Utah, 1975.)

It is my sincere prayer that the ideas and thoughts presented to you in this book will serve as a guide to this end. It is my experience, and therefore my testimony, that true happiness comes only through keeping the commandments. And that, of course, goes for happiness in dating and marriage as in all other facets of life.

137

I wish you all success and happiness as you prepare for your most perfect date.